The Castles of

An historical and architectural guide and gazetteer

R M Smith

Trearne Press, Beith, Scotland

Acknowledgements

While the impetus behind this book stems from the author's long-standing interest in the topic of both historic Galloway and Scottish castles in general, reflecting personal opinion formed from extensive reading and field-visits, nonetheless, particular sources have been relied upon in providing concise detail relating to the gazetteer entries making up two-thirds of the overall text; this primarily in respect of measurements obtained by survey (buildings and earthworks). The most frequent source consulted has been the online databases of the Royal Commission on the Ancient and Historical Monuments of Scotland (RCAHMS) - which themselves contain collated material - in addition to separately published works by other archaeologists and architectural-historians. These individuals, listed under Bibliography at the end of this book, are in the main Chris Tabraham, Richard Oram, and John Gifford. Material by Innes MacLeod has also been of assistance.

The photographs accompanying the text are from the author's own collection, while the line drawings are reproduced from the Victorian-era works of McGibbon and Ross, McKerlie, and Harper (for each see bibliography).

Cover illustrations (clockwise): Threave Castle, Castlewigg, Castle Kennedy; back cover: Kenmure Castle doorway.

ISBN 978-0-9554411-0-3

Published by Trearne Press, 23 Crummock Street,
Beith, North Ayrshire KA15 2BD

Contents

Area definition and Gazetteer notes
Historical-Architectural background

Castles in context 6

The appearance of castles in Galloway 6

Galloway's lack of 'Norman' stone castles 12

13th century castles of enclosure 13

Royal castles in Galloway 17

Episcopal castles in Galloway 18

The 14th century - rise of the tower-house 21

Threave Castle - tower-house and fortress 22

Tower-house development to c.1500 23

16th-17th century tower-houses 25

Gazetteer notes

1. West Rhins 30

2. East Rhins 37

3. Machars & Penninghame 43

4. Western Kirkcudbrightshire 57

5. Eastern Kirkcudbrightshire 70

6. Map and key 96

Postscript 92
Bibliography & further reading 93

*Lochnaw Castle
19th Century sketch,
MacGibbon & Ross
(see page 36)*

*Craichlaw: heavily
restored tower-house
(see page 46)*

Area definition and gazetteer notes

With a modern constitutional designation covering the counties of Wigtown, Kirkcudbright, and parts of Dumfriesshire, the third district falls outwith the region proper as recognised from medieval times to the 20th century. Admittedly a precise historic definition of Galloway allows for some leeway in fixing a northern boundary. Nevertheless the obvious western and southern coastline, and the Nith (or the Urr for a purely Lordship definition) before Dumfries town on the west, marked out the province in the eyes of the Scottish Crown by the mid-12th century. Accordingly, what later became the Stewartry of Kirkcudbright and Wigtownshire - the latter by c.1245 a sheriffdom in its own right - were formed as royal administrative areas based on a sub-division (with topography again a factor) of the old Lordship. Hence while the relevance of northern districts once vaguely considered Galloway (now in southern Ayrshire), or areas forming virtually a royal buffer zone immediately west, cannot be discounted from the historical introduction below, they are omitted from coverage in the gazetteer section. The latter covers the historic boundaries of Wigtownshire and Kirkcudbrightshire as understood prior to the local government alterations of 1975.

Each of the five gazetteer area guides contains entries relating to vanished castles (either medieval earthworks classed as mottes, or tower-houses - sometimes both on one site). In addition a few other earthworks are listed over which doubt exists as to medieval status; however this is stated where relevant. A number of unlikely sites some of which have been dubbed 'castle' in antiquity, have been omitted - even though future excavation (improbable at most locations) could in fact see some verified.

Inevitably many sites are situated on privately-owned ground, whether on working farms or purely residential property. Hence a 'close-up' visit may not be always be practical, or deemed permissible. An important factor here - and in general even at easily accessible buildings - is the unstable and/or dangerous condition of many structures. Most ruins are not maintained - the exemplary Historic Scotland properties forming a collective exception - and a safe rule-of-thumb would be not to enter, and certainly not climb upon, ruins.

Castles in context

Aesthetic and merely popular notions aside, the term 'castle' technically denotes a fortified centre of lordship placed at a focal point (*caput*) of lands held on the basis of military service (sometimes referred to as knight service) from the Crown. Thus the chronological starting point for British castle studies has been the mid-later 11th century, i.e. the era witnessing the introduction of the 'feudal system' into England (and gradually into Scotland) following the Norman Conquest. In recent decades some historians have challenged the radical nature of the system as it was previously understood, seeing it more as an acceleration and (by written charter) formalisation of changes already affecting land-holding in pre-Norman England. However, that the character of the landholding class was radically changed by the influx of large numbers of French (not all were 'Norman') knights is indisputable. Also evident, and important for our purpose, is that where they settled on estates (fiefs) granted them by Crown, the characteristic pudding-bowl 'motte' erected by the incomers as part of a larger earth and timber castle differed from the residence of previous, indigenous, lords, and made for a general transformation of the landscape.

The appearance of castles in Galloway

Despite a recent scholarly reassessment of Galloway's 'native' 12th century Lords - with Fergus and his heir-sons Gilbert and Uchtred now appreciated as men quite familiar with the wider 'feudalised' Anglo-French world (not least by their close contact with Henry I and Henry II of England) - the actual penetration of foreign knights into Galloway west of the Nith is still thought unlikely to have begun before 1160. Although a couple knights from a family already established in Cumbria may have been settled fractionally within Galloway (Colvend and Southwick) by Radulf. The main infeudation process however, followed the overthrow of Lord Fergus by Malcolm IV (1154-65) King of Scots, subsequent to the involvement of the enigmatic *rex Galwitensium* in what appears to have been a wider national plot. Like other peripheral regions (cumulatively the greater part of what later became Scotland proper) where royal authority was tenuous, i.e. the West Coast and the then huge province of Moray, it made common sense for the Scots kings to use the incoming knights almost as a troubleshooting police force; while at the same time including them in part of a wider agenda intended to bring their fledgling kingdom into line with western Christendom. With no local (blood-kin) ties, and holding their land in the manner of a written contract direct from the king, their loyalties were almost assured - a situation in stark contrast with native chiefs.

Charter and landscape evidences attest to the not uncommon incidence of knights receiving contiguously placed fiefs in 'frontier' zones. This situation provided mutual support (particularly military) and collectively formed a buffer zone against the semi-independent (for the most part Gaelo-Norse) lords to the West and North. A variation on this theme saw large provinces granted as single fiefs - likewise by charter for military (knight) service - from the king. These in turn would usually (in classic feudal fashion) be subdivided into smaller fiefs by the principle recipient, e.g. as surviving evidences show with regards to the fitzAlans in Renfrewshire and de Brus in Annandale

In regions where more peaceful conditions prevailed, especially in the east of the country (and particularly Lothian) smaller knight-service fiefs typically corresponded with what were (or soon became) parish units - again

Motte of Urr, 19th century panoramic view from south (Harper)

part of the overall design to strengthen Crown control. The wider feudal programme also involved a Church reorganised on the continental (i.e. Romanised) model, with additionally lands granted to monastic orders deriving from northern France. Meanwhile, the old Celtic monasteries were phased out. Important towns, in trading and/or strategic terms, became royal (or occasionally baronial) burghs - Dumfries so by the later 12th century - the number increasing as the Edinburgh-based monarchy secured more of the Scottish land mass. Justice was administered by Crown-appointed regional justiciars, or sheriffs, covering a defined district - such as Wigtownshire, seemingly established following the final (and unsuccessful) 'separatist' Galloway rebellion of 1247.

Certainly prior to the early-mid 13th century, royal control of Galloway was insufficient to establish an orderly development of the feudal programme taking place elsewhere in Lowland Scotland. The situation closer to Dumfries was doubtless more settled. But even here, the survival of few charters relating to late 12th century infeudation - the situation is worse west of the Dee - presents a major obstacle to working out any feudal 'map' (something which can be conjectured in much of Annandale, Renfrewshire, and Lothian). Yet, despite usually drawing a cartulary blank, several classic and symbolic pairings of motte and adjacent parish kirk (the latter all since rebuilt) can be seen today in the neighbouring parishes of St John's Town of Dalry, Balmaclellan, and Parton - on the east side of the Ken and bordering less hospitable and barren lands to the West. Similar, if less obvious, motte clusters appear in southern Kirkcudbrightshire, and (see below) on the eastern shore of the Wigtownshire Rhins.

Charter evidence directly links the huge motte complex at Urr with Hugh de Berkeley, an aristocratic knight granted lands there soon after 1160 by Uchtred. Holding effectively most of his father Fergus's forfeited lordship from the Crown, Uchtred proved the most amenable of the half-brothers to Scottish (at the time, an appellation not applied to the inhabitants of Galloway) royal control. This grant, and another of Borgue to Hugh de Moreville, again reflected standard practice in the feudal landholding pyramid. There are, however, only similarly sure evidences for another four or so Galloway mottes - with a handful of others inferable - out of a number somewhere in the region of eighty.

Chronicle and supporting archaeological evidences testify to an 1174 rebellion in Galloway against the Scottish royal overlord - and by implication the resented Anglo-French incomers - by Gilbert (*Gillebrigte*) lord from probably even before 1160 of the territories west of the Cree (more or less what became Wigtownshire), where the indigenous landholding class had remained in local control. Uchtred too may have been involved in the uprising, despite later portrayals of him as a 'true Scot' remaining loyal to the king. However Gilbert had him almost immediately killed, evidently desiring the title Lord of Galloway to himself in the manner of his father Fergus.

Typical tree-covered motte today, here at Parton

Again, traditional portrayals of this as an anti-feudal backlash now seem an over simplification, yet contain much truth. The chronicle of Roger of Howden recounts how the Galwegians:

> expelled from Galloway all the bailiffs and wardens whom the king of Scotland had set over them; and all the English and French whom they could seize they slaughtered; and all the fortifications and castles which the king of Scotland had established in their land they besieged, took and levelled , . . .

Native resentment and desire for revenge were doubtless motivating factors; while it is clear the principal targets were mottes such as de Berkeley's at Urr - where archaeological evidence of destruction is dated to this time. Moreover, it was no mere coincidence that the rebellion began during a period of crisis for the Scottish Crown, i.e. the capture by Henry II of

England of King William 'the Lion'. Gilbert even offered to accept the more powerful English king (to whom he was related - Fergus having previously married an illegitimate daughter of Henry I) as overlord - a clever calculation, as it may have served to ward off an inevitable Scottish re-invasion of Galloway; while English overlordship in the distant region would be little more than token, and Galloway effectively independent.

It seems probable, though not beyond dispute (see below), that the majority if not all mottes lying within present day Wigtownshire date from the subjugation of Gilbert's own territory following his death in 1185. A virtual line of mottes on the east shore of the Rhins is suggestive of a systematic 'planting' of incoming knights. The victorious invader was Roland (*Lachlan*), son of the murdered Uchtred, whose army probably contained a sizeable portion of Anglo-French knights, and who came with tacit Crown approval (and possibly armed support). Only two resulting Wigtownshire mottes can be clearly identified by surviving charter/chronicle evidence: that of Sorbie granted to the de Vieuxponts by Roland soon after the conquest; and the dramatically sited cliff top 'motte' at Cruggleton (on the east coast of the Machars), caput of an estate created by Roland for himself. Excavation has established this naturally strategic site as a far earlier centre of lordship. Defence aside, the continuity was poignant and symbolic. Moreover the site was only a few miles north of the already important ecclesiastical centre of Whithorn - where Roland's grandfather Fergus probably established an Augustinian priory at an existing monastery.

While the huge motte and bailey complex at Urr, along with more modest examples like Sorbie, were almost entirely artificial 'textbook' examples, many more like Borgue and notably Cruggleton utilised natural features such as rock face or a promontory headland (both in the latter case). The topography of regions like Galloway leant itself well to such solutions, unlike for example the low lying fertile plains of southern and midland England which the Normans had dotted with 'standard-edition' mottes in the years following the 1066 Conquest. In fact, such a heterogeneous range of sites and structures apparently served the incoming knights as castles - including it seems at least one twin crannog site (excavated at Lochrutton) - that without further excavation it is nigh impossible to distinguish many sites representing knight-service fiefs from what were more likely sites of indigenous lordship. Indeed Lochrutton, Buittle and other places may indicate a simple transferral of ownership - with any degree of rebuilding or modification varying, and not necessarily undertaken immediately.

Conversely, there seems no reason why Gilbert or even Fergus, given their familiarity with Norman and in turn Angevin England, could not have

built their very own showpiece 'modern' castles. The large and strategically sited Wigtownshire motte and bailey of Innermessan (which appears to overlie an earlier lordship site) could represent such an undertaking. Yet by the same token, it, and others, may represent post 1185 colonisation.

Cruggleton Castle, as depicted in the 16th century

Certainly, Fergus is reputed to have constructed a motte on a site now within Kirkcudbright town ('Moat Brae'), 0.75 miles from his existing caput of 'Fergus Isle' lying outwith the settlement. By the 13th century some native families who had retained, or newly acquired, land were probably adopting the motte form. This may explain the absence of defensive baileys - a generic term for a defensive basecourt, few of which survive even in earthwork form - at many sites (at others they have simply disappeared), Pulcree and Little Duchrae being possible examples in this category. Some castle-historians of late have suggested a clear lack of bailey points to native construction, as the feature served as almost a fortified barrack in hostile territory. Adding to the confusion, and in further reference to smaller sites largely formed from natural features, enthusiastic antiquarians of recent (typically 19th century) times identified several former 'mottes' that now appear natural in their entirety, with no hint of having undergone medieval occupation, e.g. Horse Hill (NX 144556; a sand dune at Luce Sands - certainly formed like a motte), Ballochadee (NX 296656) and 'Moat

Plantation' (NX 357674). Debate now even surrounds the 'classic' Wigtownshire motte of Droughdool, where recent excavation has suggested purely pre-medieval use.

National and regional (Galloway) lack of 'Norman' stone castles

Yet another former axiom of Scottish castle studies, namely that by the later 13th century earth and timber castles had become redundant as fortresses, has been revised largely by the findings of archaeology. Mottes are now understood to have been constructed as late as c.1300. Although, in the majority of cases the original timber tower - from say a late 12th century motte - would simply be repaired or replaced over the course of time. Meanwhile, ancillary structures on and around the site (i.e. within the bailey) likewise frequently remained of wood until the later 14th or even 15th century. By this later period, however, they began to replaced as standard by an adjacent or nearby stone tower-house (of which more below) and barmkin.

It can seem puzzling that the large-scale transition from earth-and-timber motte and bailey to stone keep and attached stone enclosure, seen throughout England and the subjugated areas of Wales by the early 12th century, was not replicated afterwards in Scotland. A fair proportion of Scotland's Anglo-French incomers clearly had the wealth to copy their southern counterparts. Meanwhile, and in emulation of the Crown, the patronage given the new monastic orders by the same families (and by some native magnates such as Fergus) in the mid-later 12th century, not to mention the importation of skilled labour to construct the abbeys and priories, showed the importance they placed on prestige and 'modernity' in other respects.

Yet no single tower of the type mentioned - or even sound archaeological evidence of one - is known to have existed in Scotland. Piecemeal evidences suggest keeps and/or stone enclosure castles in existence by the early 12th century at the royal fortresses of Edinburgh, Invergowrie, Roxburgh, and possibly elsewhere. It would hardly be surprising if the MacMalcom (Canmore-dynasty) monarchs, especially the anglicised David I (1124-53), wished their own versions of the huge Norman keeps appearing before 1100 in England (notably at London, Colchester and Rochester). David is in fact credited with beginning the stone keep at Carlisle, then in Scots-held territory.

Droughdool, a 'motte' now under question

However, if royal evidences are fragmentary and highly conjectural, the picture is still bleaker with regard to the castles of 12th century Scotland's Anglo-French nobility. This is clear in Galloway, where at the huge mottes mentioned no indication of original stone walling has been found.

Galloway's 'lost' fortresses - 13th century stone castles of enclosure

Nevertheless, one aspect of Scotland's castle heritage now receiving a more positive reassessment concerns the nation's stone castles of enclosure, sometimes termed 'courtyard' castles, or castles of *enceinte*. In England, and again in subjugated Wales and Ireland, this type of castle - some versions of which appeared only marginally different from the keep and curtain wall (not least to their incorporation of earlier work - rendering castle 'categorisation' a problematic business) became standard by the mid-13th century. In theory, defensive strength was balanced out through mutually supporting towers, and usually also a twin-towered gatehouse. The form found its apogee in the huge concentric (or near concentric) castles built by Edward I in Wales. Yet in origin the features and concept of the enclosure castle (like the motte) were imported from France, with castle historians having noted the direct influence of French castles like Coucy in Scotland during the northern kingdom's 'Golden Age'.

It is commonly appreciated that during this peaceful and prosperous era, largely concurrent with the reign of Alexander III (1249-86), the feudalised kingdom's stock of castles, previously dismal by Southern comparison, was greatly enhanced by a series of impressive courtyard castles built by men regarded as having been 'second-tier' yet aspiring nobles of Anglo-French descent. The impressive ruins surviving at Direlton and Bothwell (both inviting the Coucy comparison), and to a lesser extent Caerlaverock, exemplify the group. Certainly a range of small and compact, but comparatively featureless, stone enclosure castles had appeared on the Gaelo-Norse controlled western seaboard by around c.1200. However, these lay in a region beyond *de facto* Scottish Crown control. Only the fitz Alan's shell-keep of Rothesay (modelled on English examples, and in dating from c.1200 perhaps representing an extant 'first' in this respect) on the Isle of Bute possibly represents the first visible 'bridgehead' of the new feudal order into Gaeldom. Yet combined evidences now seem to suggest that there may well have been far more impressive courtyard castles than is readily appreciated, the majority of these being the castles famously destroyed by the Scots during the Wars of Independence.

Galloway, along with adjacent parts of Dumfriesshire, would certainly appear to substantiate the theory in regional terms. This is due not least to lands (and hence castles) that had come to be held in the region by important magnates who became bitter enemies of Robert Bruce, notably in this sense the traditionally vilified Baliols and Comyns (like Bruce, originally *de Brus*, again of Anglo-French origin). Following the death of Alan, Lord of Galloway in 1234, Alexander II (1214-49) was able to divide the lordship between Alan's three daughter-heirs. Another rebellion, this time in support of Alan's illegitimate son Thomas, and again characterised as a 'Celtic' backlash (Thomas may well have received support from kindred Gaelo-Norse elements in Man, Ulster and the Isles) was put down - a near-lifetime imprisonment in royal, then Baliol, castles being accorded to Thomas 'the bastard' (until released aged eighty-eight by Edward I of England in a bizarre propaganda ploy!).

Of the three magnate-husbands of Alan's heirs, one - William de Forz - died without issue, the lands held by him and Christina being seemingly divided between the other two. These men, Roger de Quincy, Earl of Winchester, and John Baliol (whose estates included Barnard castle near

c.1300 Baliol castle of Loch Doon, before removal to shore (MacGibbon & Ross)

Durham) became responsible for most of present day Wigtownshire and Kirkcudbrightshire respectively - although there was no exact geographical division, with some Baliol estates lying west of the Cree and vice versa. Each administered their lordships from existing centres, Cruggleton and either Buittle or (more likely at first) Burned Island on Loch Ken. With extensive lands and castles elsewhere, perhaps neither man felt any need to immediately construct a showpiece castle in what they likely considered a quite remote (and recently 'conquered') part of the realm. Yet any resumption of archaeological excavation at Buittle (halted short of the 'motte'/inner ward) may well reveal a stone curtain wall from this period - the gatehouse remains are certainly mid-later 13th century. Nonetheless it seems probable that his widow Devorgilla - who evidently spent much time at the castle and was responsible for the magnificent Cistercian abbey of Sweetheart, undertook the main rebuilding at Buittle following John Baliol's death.

An inspection of what might be termed the inner ward at Buittle (heavily overgrown, so best viewed in winter) immediately encounters the lower portions of a twin-towered gatehouse and drawbridge-pit. The structure contained fine ashlar work, as seen at Caerlaverock (where the upper portions of the present gatehouse represent 14th-15th century rebuilding), the dimensions being approximately the same as the triangular stronghold. Buittle's form though, was more irregular - possibly oval; but the near encircling river Urr and an intersecting ditch may have provided, as at Caerlaverock, a complete water defence.

At Cruggleton, Alexander Comyn, Earl of Buchan, replaced his late father-in-law Roger de Quincy following the latter's death in 1264. The Comyns were probably the most powerful family in 13th century Scotland, trusted Crown agents whose various lands bordering the insecure north-west were guarded by sizeable stone castles surviving notably at Balvenie, Lochindorb and Inverlochy. Alexander's cousin, John Comyn of Badenoch, was by this time already in possession of lands centred on Dalswinton in Dumfriesshire.

Buittle Castle, inner ward (gatehouse remains in centre)

Late 18th century accounts record the recent survival of sections of stone wall at Dalswinton some 12-14 feet in width; these remains were quarried in 1785, and later the area landscaped (it was recently a tennis court). An antiquarian print survives of Dalswinton before complete demolition, but scale cannot be reliably ascertained from such drawings.

Other once major stone castles of 13th lordship fringing Galloway can be found at Auchencass (near Moffat), where lower portions of a quadrangular enclosure with circular corner tower and extensive earthworks survive; and at Tibbers, where a similar plan had a form of twin-towered gatehouse at one angle. Conforming to the usual sequence, both these thirteenth century stone castles replaced earlier mottes. Tibbers, a largely natural promontory-motte, utilised the same site. Less impressive but earlier, the recently excavated c.1220 first stone castle at Caerlaverock was rather crude in design, even following the addition of corner towers after a decade or so (the whole was then abandoned for the present castle 200m to the north by c.1270). Much further north, fractionally into present day Ayrshire yet historic Galloway territory, the diminutive but remarkable eleven-sided c.1300 Baliol island castle of Loch Doon has lost its former presence by being rebuilt on shore in the 1930s. By the era of Loch Doon's construction, Baliol days of peace and prosperity had been in decline since the death of Alexander III (d.1286); this partly explains its near-inaccessible location and those of subsequent island sites occupied by the Baliols in following half-century (Hestan Island and a re-occupation of Burned Island), where apparently very basic castles were built.

Royal castles in Galloway

A castle was probably built by the Crown at Dumfries in the late 12th century, during which years direct control of Lower Nithsdale was assumed following the death of the 'friendly' native lord, Radulf, and the probable imposition of a sheriff (perhaps one Roger de Minto). Placed almost on the Nith, it was, given royal designs on Galloway proper, a strategic and symbolic position - and had direct access to the sea. The now landscaped/defaced but huge earthworks within Castle Dykes park testify to the scale of the fortress. While David I (1124-53) had built in stone thirty miles away at Carlisle Castle, the late 12th century castle at Dumfries was however probably only of earth and timber. Yet based on precedents elsewhere (and on information gleaned from exchequer rolls), it was most likely re-erected in stone during the reign of Alexander III. It does not seem unreasonable to posit for Dumfries all the usual components of a large courtyard castle: towers, a *donjon* (tower-keep) and a twin-towered gateway.

More is known concerning the layout of a smaller royal stone castle at Kirkcudbright, in part due to extensive surviving earthworks, but more importantly due to an excavation conducted within these in 1911-13. Similar to Dumfries, the first castle at Kirkcudbright 'Castledykes' was probably a later 12th century variation on the motte and bailey, with again its inner ward rebuilt around a century later in stone. The archaeologists unearthed a twin-towered gateway with projecting buttresses and three wall towers, one of which was particularly large and presumably intended to serve as a *donjon*.

At Wigtown, mentioned as a royal burgh in 1292 but in probability already one for decades, a castle served as the centre of the sheriffdom of Wigtownshire (most likely created following the 1247 rebellion). The site is in an unusually low position beneath the town. However, a much later diversion of the River Bladnoch - at the mouth of which the castle once stood - has resulted in the present location 200m or so inland, belying its original strategic situation. Again a ditch was apparently cut to give all-round water defence. The structure was another apparently destroyed during the Wars of Independence, its stones being quarried for centuries thereafter (as late as the 1820s in the construction of a nearby harbour). But a close inspection reveals hollows indicating a twin-towered gatehouse on the western side of the former courtyard.

Episcopal castles

The 12th century reorganisation of the Church on continental (Roman) lines was in a sense a pragmatic move by the Scottish Crown. The 'new' and uniform belief system served as an indirect extension of royal authority; not least because bishops in the new (or restructured) dioceses tended to be royal appointees. Educated men were scarce outside the Church; with in particular the monastic houses connected with the new system regarded as beacons of learning. Individual Bishops were moreover usually wealthy landowners; all in all, powerful figures even in purely secular terms. Therefore it seems hardly surprising to find them typically having two or more defensive residences within diocese bounds (one sometimes termed a 'winter palace').

Subsequent urban development at most former episcopal towns, and redundancy of use following the Reformation, are factors explaining the disappearance of most bishop's castles. Nonetheless, the favoured castle-type now known (largely as a result of excavation) to have existed at most 12th-13th century locations was the ringwork - a variation on the motte. Lower, and with a larger surface area than a motte, a ringwork afforded some degree of protection but would have been more conducive to comfort and the placing of a spacious timber hall-complex, all within a palisade. Neither would it have physically dominated an adjacent cathedral (often quite small affairs in the 12th century), nor had overt military associations. The castle site associated with the Bishops of Whithorn (Balnespik) may well have been a ringwork. No trace of earthworks remain, though indeed the mere filling of an encircling ditch by later farmers (Balnespik now lies within a field) could account for this; while infinitely more work would be required to remove a motte mound. Certainly, earth and timber ringwork castles appeared next to opulent new stone churches at 12th century Glasgow, St Andrew's, and elsewhere. The restoration of the Galloway bishopric in the mid-12th century, marked by the erection of a fine Romanesque church, could indicate another instance of the grouping. West of the Cree, in Girthon parish, the large ditched enclosure of 'Palace Yard' has been tentatively suggested as an episcopal residence; though there is no documentary evidence to support the theory.

Of the quadrangular stone courtyard castles that seem to have characterised bishop's castles from the late 13th century (again mostly disappeared, e.g. Glasgow, Aberdeen, Fetternear, Dunkeld; St Andrew's surviving in rebuilt form), in Galloway traces of stone and an outline of a ditch at the noted episcopal centre of Penninghame possibly indicate the former presence of a small version of the type. This site, known as Penninghame Hall, is tellingly located on the Bishops Burn. Finally, on the conjectural topic of this type of defensive structure: of the large tower houses associated with many bishops in the later medieval period, seen for example today at the massive Spynie (Moray) and at Carnasserie (Argyll), it is possible a variation on the type may have built at Clary (in the Penninghame locale).

Wigtown castle site; note depression indicating ditch (left-centre)

Castle Stewart

The fourteenth century - decline of the courtyard castle and rise of the tower-house

During the Wars of Independence prior to Bannockburn (1314), and intermittently from the 1330s until the mid-century, occupying English soldiers had been able maintain a hold - if an increasingly tenuous one - over much of Lowland Scotland by occupying key castles. Usually these were the royal and sometimes also baronial stone courtyard castles built during the reigns of Alexander II and III. The ironic lesson was not lost on Bruce's men during the 1300s, who on capturing an English-held fortress would normally render it incapable of future defence by 'slighting' - the degree of which varied from place to place. In Galloway, this process accounted for the royal castles of Dumfries (later accounts of Dumfries castle probably refer to one of the town's several mottes, or a smaller structure constructed post-1314 on the castle ruins), Kirkcudbright and Wigtown, all of which were never rebuilt and whose urban location ensured subsequent quarry use (and hence disappearance beyond earthworks).

Perhaps more poignantly, the power held in the region by Bruce's arch-enemies, the Comyns and Baliols (both effectively forced to acquiesce in English rule after 1296 - thereafter to be dubbed collaborators in popular history) saw their castles of Cruggleton, Dalswinton and Buittle accorded the same treatment. A 'native' largely Wigtownshire-based family, the MacDowalls, proved more stubborn enemies of Bruce (whose soldiers were, after all, 'invaders') than either Baliol or Comyn. However, their relative unimportance in national terms, their lack of large castles and perhaps also the fact of some branches of the family apparently supporting Bruce, seem to have been factors combining to ensure their survival as landholders following the Wars of Independence. A similar story applies to the McCullochs and MacLellans.

The majority of the large stone castles demolished in the 1300s were simply left as ruins. Reasons that help explain this include conditions decidedly lacking peace and prosperity (rebuilding such structures was a costly and lengthy business) - not least because the Wars with England continued periodically for decades. Moreover many of the estates had been given as reward to 'patriots' who supported Bruce, with the likes of Baliols and Comyns forfeited and often in exile. Some old sites may even have been regarded as tainted; but for all practical purposes tended to pose too great a challenge to reconstruct. A few strategic royal castles were repaired and strengthened, such as Edinburgh and Stirling, but not Dumfries; while a number of baronial castles (especially those held pre-c.1300 by pro-Bruce families) damaged by English armies were repaired and soon augmented (e.g. Bothwell, held by de Moray; Kildrummy, Earl of Mar; and Caerlaverock, the principle stronghold of the somewhat less reliable Maxwells).

These factors, and what can now be perceived as a distinctive architectural trend in castle-building, by the mid-14th century seem to have prompted the beginning of what would become a three-century Scottish pre-occupation with the tower-house. One even appeared as the centrepiece of the rebuilt Edinburgh Castle ('David's Tower' - the foundations of which survive). Earlier, plain stone towers had formed the main component of promontory castles in 12th century Norse-controlled Caithness and Orkney. Plain tower-keeps subsequently appeared in Lowland areas during the later 13th and early 14th centuries. Although it would seem that the favoured type of stone castle constructed during this era, especially by lower-ranking knights, was the hall-house. Lower and more elongated than tower-houses, fragments of these stone halls survive in Galloway at Lochnaw and Mochrum (both island sites), and more substantially in Dumfriesshire at Morton Castle. Recent archaeology has shown that on briefly re-occupying Buittle in the mid-14th century, the Baliols may have constructed a stone hall in the former bailey of their slighted courtyard castle. However, almost immediate expulsion saw the lands returned again to the Douglases, who in the person of Sir James Douglas had already received them from his uncle, King Robert I (Bruce), a decade or so after Bannockburn.

Threave castle - tower-house and fortress

The very conditions that appear to have combined to bring about the appearance of the tower-house as a dominant element in the Scottish landscape by the mid-later 14th century, perhaps find no better exemplification in Scotland than witnessed today at Threave Castle, sited on a small island in the River Dee. The builder was Archibald Douglas (the

'Grim'), whose family had fought on the side of Bruce and were accordingly rewarded with forfeited lands. In addition to raising a massive rectangular tower of serious defensive capability, Archibald chose a centrally located (in regional Galloway terms) but isolated setting on an island - which of course would multiply difficulties for any intending besieging force. The tower formerly had considerable ancillary (domestic and service) accommodation in the form of adjacent halls, recently revealed by archaeological excavation. A similar scenario existed at most if not all tower-houses, but again few remnants of these ranges (usually contained within a small courtyard wall - or 'barmkin') can be seen today; later remodelling and additions, the removal of stones for farm buildings, etc., having accounted for most. However, at Threave these buildings were apparently cleared within the first century of the castle's construction - in order to give a clear field of fire to a remarkable artillery fortification built around the base of the tower. Dated to c.1450, it is contemporary with James II's artillery-blockhouse of Ravenscraig Castle in Fife and testimony in itself to the Douglases' power, awareness of the latest developments in continental fortification, and probably also their realisation of a looming showdown with the Crown.

By the later 15th century two dozen or so tower-houses dotted the region (though none with the presence or defensive capability of Threave) representing most of the principal and some lesser families. These included the unique Orchardton, built in a circular plan (normally only found in Ireland). The number would soon multiply.

Tower-house development to c.1500

A practical (and commonly seen today) tower-house feature was structural strengthening obtained by vaulting the ground floor. At Cruggleton, a portion of this (reinforced in recent times) is all that remains of an late 14th century tower-house constructed on the 'motte' of the castle slighted in 1308. The Cruggleton re-builders were either Douglases or a Prior of Whithorn. At ground-floor level, storage space and often a kitchen was provided, the overarching vault being frequently subdivided by a wooden floor (the upper level being referred to as an entresol). The floors above were almost always reached by a stone turnpike stair contained in the wall thickness of one corner; although occasionally the only communication from ground to first (or at least basement to entresol) level was through a hatch. Somewhat grimly, and evident at Threave and other Galloway tower-houses dating from the medieval era, a pit prison was contained in one corner entered from a trapdoor above (sometimes located in a slightly more 'comfortable' cell). Not surprisingly, the lower floor of the castle had few external openings, walls commonly being 2m in width (more at Threave), and had the main doorway often placed at entresol or first-floor level. A timber stair leading to this could be removed in times of danger.

Almost as a rule the first-floor contained the castle's main hall, graced by a large fireplace often ornately carved. This can be seen in fragments at Cardoness (a sizeable rectangular tower built by the McCullochs c.1470) and other locations. At second and third floor levels, the lord's private-domestic quarters were floored in timber and sometimes divided into separate rooms by wooden screens (like the floors, now almost always gone) and typically well provided with aumbries, garderobe closets, stone benches set in window embrasures (the same, but larger, usually also featuring in the hall); and of course the household fittings, which added comfort to what today can appear bare and unappealing abodes.

At Threave and Cardoness, plain battlemented parapets were intended to give complete wallhead defence. The former contained a low attic within, intended to house a siege-garrison when needed - openings in the parapet giving access to another (if temporary and removable) defensive feature in the form of an overhanging wooden hoarding. It was probably never put to use - Threave's two sieges were apparently decided by artillery fire from long-range (not to mention some honourable concessions granted the besieged). And in fact the lord's apartments on the two floors beneath were unlikely to have been regularly disturbed by soldiers ascending and descending the common turnpike stair. A more usual feature seen by the 15th century was the placing of a gabled attic within the parapet, for example at Cardoness and Rusco (built by the Gordons). Decorative features adorning towers by c.1500 included corbels (intended to give the effect of an overhanging parapet) set singly or in more elaborate formations, and roundels formed at parapet angles. Cardoness had neither, Rusco has corbelling, with both features appear at the fragmentary Myrton (built by another branch of the McCullochs) and the intact Lochnaw (Agnew) of c.1500 and c.1470 respectively.

These latest trends in architectural embellishment were adopted as standard by builders with any pretension as men of (even local) importance, though are less apparent today due to the survival of few towers in Galloway to wallhead level. Conversely, the commonplace survival of lower (in most places at least ground) floor can reveal the cost-saving device employed at a few towers of dispensing with a stone vault, e.g. Cumstoun and the more extant Castle Stewart.

Sixteenth-seventeenth century tower-houses.

Before the end of 15th century tower-houses were appearing in 'L-plan' form. This design normally allowed a stair to be placed in a short wing ('jamb') leading to the first-floor hall, extra accommodation usually placed above this, while (in a mid-later 16th development) the turnpike would continue in a projecting semi-turret in the re-entrant angle. St John's Castle, Stranraer, of c.1510 is probably the earliest (certainly surviving, though altered) example of an L-plan tower-house in Galloway. However, variations on the type became commonplace as tower-houses proliferated - with even landowners of fairly modest means ('bonnet lairds' and cadet branches of established families) keen to achieve the status associated with the stylish residences. This process was accelerated by the distribution of Church lands at the Reformation, but did not stem from it.

Rather than demolish and wholly replace an existing earlier tower (i.e. of rectangular form), sometimes a wing was attached, attaining the desired effect at a fraction of the cost. This appears to have been the case at the surviving tower-houses of Carsluith (with some debate, or at least the time-lag between the two sections uncertain), Barholm, and Buittle Place - though harling coating the latter two buildings covers the tell-tale change in masonry. Sixteenth century L-plan towers of one-stage build are numerous, with extant examples including: Dunskey (though like others following, with later additions), Galdenoch, Castle of Park, Castlewigg, Sorbie, Plunton, MacLellan's (an elaborate variation) and Drumcoltran. Yet at Craigcaffie, in the 1570s, the builder seemed content to erect in the old rectangular style.

Rusco Castle, 19th c. print (Harper)

Intermittent warfare and feuding, at both national and local level, in 16th century Scotland undoubtedly prolonged the life of the castle - albeit in tower-house form - at a time when landed families in more peaceful and stable England were living in homes where comfort, space and other purely domestic or aesthetic concerns were almost the only considerations in design. Moreover, the martial traditions of families north of the Border (Scottish armies could not afford the professional soldiery increasingly used by the Tudors) fostered continued notions of a castle-like home. Hence while it is often suggested that the gun loops placed especially around the lower floors of many 16th and even 17th century buildings were intended for purely decorative (including symbolic) effect, an accompanying scarcity of windows (other than slits) at this level and the standard placing of one gunloop flanking the doorway indicate some intention as a security measure. Certainly not one intended to repulse a besieging army (an unlikely event), but perhaps useful if threatened by a smaller force. The decades after c.1540 witnessed wars involving England which became increasingly complex, involving interacting concerns of civil war, religious strife, and even imported French troops.

Some of the tower-houses built towards the end of the century were quite sumptuous affairs - MacLellan's Castle in Kirkcudbright town perhaps being the prime example; with Sorbie (though of inferior stonework) another of note. Each was constructed with a scale-and-platt stairway (instead of the standard turnpike) leading to the hall. Popular variations on the L-plan were the T-plan and the Z-plan, each of which saw the old rectangular block supplemented with two short wings/jambs (in the Z-plan these would be off-set from the main block, and appear as towers in their own right). Few of either, however, appear to have been built in the region, but are represented at the Old Place of Monreith and a (badly ruined) Auchenskeoch respectively.

*Dunskey Castle, view over cliffs
(McGibbon & Ross)*

The tower-house tradition in fact continued until the mid-later 17th century, though many buildings began to look more like prototype mansion houses. Castle Kennedy of c.1600 seems to conveniently form a watershed in this respect. Yet despite a 'new' form approximating to the letter 'Y', its effect was still vertical, while gunloops continued to feature at ground level and above. Dunskey was remodelled with a new stair, and given a feature which became common in the form of a long and low attached wing; but again it was planned in a security-concious manner on what was already a naturally defensive site. Similarly, the c.1630 wing attached to the tower-house at Kenmure carried gunloops along its base. Occasionally the new portion was detached, as originally at Kirkconnel House and the Old Place of Mochrum - but later filled in as these and many other tower-houses received additions and alterations in Georgian and Victorian times (and in places even into the early twentieth century). Usually in these cases the tower-house was preserved - again not least for symbolic purposes - without excessive alteration. Although where later mansions incorporated already-ruined towers, the latter might be 'sympathetically' reconstructed, e.g. Craichlaw; and famously at the Old Place of Mochrum. At some locations later wings have been since removed, e.g. Lochnaw and Earlstoun.

The later 17th century witnessed the final stage of what might conceivably still be called castle building in Scotland. A new L-plan tower-house was built from scratch at the Isle of Whithorn. Meanwhile in the above-mentioned sequence at Old Place of Mochrum, a T-plan tower was constructed adjacent to, but separate from, the existing (15th century) one. The fragmentary remains of Carscreugh give little indication of a U-plan mansion built there around 1670; again it was a structure of considerable height. Slightly earlier than either, the T-plan Barscobe was lower in profile, but here and at the others, ground floor windows were kept small or barred, with shotholes (whether for 'decoration' or not) occasionally appearing.

Carscreugh Plan

Old Place of Mochrum (before c.1900 additions), 17th century tower on left

28

Gazetteer sections

As noted in the introductory chapter, a plethora of sites exist where medieval occupation or re-occupation (of earlier defensive residences) may have occurred, but without excavation is something remaining uncertain. The tendency in the gazetteer has been to avoid such highly dubious and undocumented sites - though the rule is not consistent, especially in regard of addressing the likelihood of sites previously listed as mottes. The surveys undertaken in recent decades by the RCAHMS and Chris Tabraham's Stewartry survey (see bibliography) in particular, have provided the main source of information in this area. There are doubtless dozens of small medieval lordship centres 'lost' within the wider category of 'miscellaneous earthworks'; however, to list all would add greatly to an existing confusion.

The Ordnance Survey Map references are intended for quick reference in conjunction with the respective 1:50 000 and 1:25 000 area sheets, recently republished in Landranger and Explorer form respectively.

Old Place of Monreith (the 'Dowies')

Wigtownshire - West Rhins

Ardwell motte (NX 107455) and castle site (NX 102455?)

An unmistakable motte on a ridge above the shore, now situated within the policies of Ardwell House. Remaining to a height of approximately 7m with a summit area of 21m, a ditch some 10m wide and 1m deep survives on two sides. Some 50m to the south of the motte are traces of another ditch and bank - probably indicating a bailey. A 'house of Ardwell', apparently standing in the 15th century and probably built by the McCullochs, has vanished. It may underlie the present 18th-19th century mansion.

Auchneight - castle site (NX 110334)

There are now no indications of the 'large and strong building' formerly standing near Auchneight farmstead, seemingly used by the McCullochs of Clanyard as a hunting lodge in the 17th century.

Auchness Castle (NX 106447)

A late rectangular tower-house, still inhabited, has been considerably enlarged and modified.

Balgreggan motte (NX 096505) and castle site (NX 089500?)

The most northernly in the line of mottes on the East Rhins shore, here a prominent position resulted in utilisation (and damage) by the Royal Observer Corps during the Second World War. Now surviving to some 8.7m, with an oval summit measuring 20m by 17m, and traces of ditch and bank. Again a later tower - as at Ardwell and seen elsewhere in Galloway (e.g. Sorbie, Castle Stewart) - eventually superseded the motte's timber hall. But like Ardwell it too has vanished. A still later house on or near the site has also gone. The MacDowalls are connected with at least the tower-house phases.

Balsarroch house (NW 994691)

Remains of a 17th century laird's house, situated some 500m S of Cairnbowie farmhouse. The two-storey house has formed the W side of a courtyard approximately 18m square. On the N side of the courtyard is an arched opening, with remains of another structure on the E.

Balzieland Castle (NX 096426)

Incorporated in a wall of the famed gardens at Logan House (itself of c.1700 and later build; with, as at Lochnaw, 19th century additions now removed), are fragments of a tower containing some window jambs built probably by the MacDowalls. It may represent the tower known to have been burnt in 1500.

Broadwall - castle site (NX 130333)

Castle Ban motte (NW 966678)

A motte scarped from a promontory stands on the coast 1 km from Mains of Airlies farm. Approximately 11.5m high on the W but now sloping to some 5m on the E, an oval summit measures around 20m in diameter. A ditch, containing a causeway over 3m wide, cuts off the landward approach. The latter is 12m broad, and now some 3 deep, with signs of a counterscarp bank.

Castle Clanyard (NX 109374)

Remains of a tower built by the Gordons of Clanyard, probably in the later 16th century and known to have been ruinous by 1684. The substantial surviving portion is the W gable, standing to some 6m in height. An armorial panel from the tower was later reset in a nearby barn.

Corsewall Castle (NW 991714)

A tower of 15th century date, originally surrounded (with its presumably disappeared barmkin) by an extensive ditch now only visible as a cropmark. Walls up to 2.5m in width rising from a plinth indicate the serious consideration given defence. Of the three floors and garret, the vaulted ground floor (7.8m by 3.5m) with entrance and part of the first floor and mural stair remain.

Craigoch Castle (NX 012668)

The elevated site of these indistinct remains have prompted suggestions of an Early Historic period Dun; certainly it is known elsewhere for such to have been reused as a medieval defence (e.g. Dun Lagaidh, Skye). Regardless, the featureless rubble walls, now only surviving to a height of at most 0.5m, indicate a former structure measuring some 14.5m by 17m.

Dunaldboys motte (NX 021518)

Here a natural eminence on the head of sea cliffs south of Knockinaam was fashioned to form a motte, now standing to some 8m-9m high. A terrace appears to have been cut into the E side, on the external side of which is a low bank. A ditch, with signs of a causeway, and the sea cliffs defend the other sides.

Dunskey Castle (NX 004534)

Sited on the head of a precipitous coastal promontory, this is one of Galloway's finest and most interesting ruins, and perhaps the most picturesque. The Adairs first had a castle here in the 14th century; although the site may have already been in occupation for centuries. The McCullochs and MacDowalls destroyed this structure in the late 1400s; however it was rebuilt in the early 16th century in the form of a large L-plan tower -house (measuring 30m by 14.5m) with a vaulted basement as standard. The entrance was later altered (possibly around c.1600) to accommodate a scale-and-platt staircase.

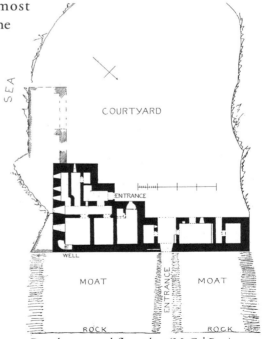

Dunskey, ground-floor plan (McG&Ross)

Dunskey Castle, view from east

Above the doorway is a triple frame indentation once housing armorial panels. A long wing projects from the N side of the tower, providing further accommodation and cutting of the landward approach. Spacious first-floor hall with fireplace and turnpike stair leading to upper storeys. The gallery-wing, of probable early 17th century date, was of two floors and an attic. The main floor of this addition is pierced by large windows; serious attack perhaps being deemed unlikely by this era - yet the exterior was protected by a 15m wide by 2.5m deep rock-cut ditch (most likely representing a 14th century or earlier undertaking). A vaulted entrance with flanking windowless guardroom passes through the wing. Fragments of walling along the cliff edge - which could have required little defending save from the stealthiest surprise attack - may contain stone from the Adairs first castle.

Drummore - castle site (NX 135364)

The surviving vaulted lower portion of a tower-house of probable 16th century date was pulled down in the early 1960s.

Galdenoch Castle (NW 974632)

At the end of a farm road, the shell of a rubble-built L-plan tower-house, looking somewhat precarious (dressed stones seem to have been mostly removed), stands adjacent to a farmhouse. Built for Gilbert Agnew of Lochnaw in the 16th century, it consists of three storeys and a garret. A roundel projects on corbelling from the SW angle. The interior dimensions measure approximately 7m

Galdenoch

by 4.5m in the main block, within walls 1m and more thick. The jamb contains remains of a turnpike stair.

Garthland - castle site (NX 077554)

Just north of the farmhouse of Garthland is the site of a probable 16th century tower-house built by the MacDowalls. Demolished in the mid-19th century, its stones were presumably used in later farm buildings. Three of these, each with a roll-moudling, are incorporated at the SE angle of a barn.

Glen-of-the-hole - castle site (NX 107370)

Approximately 120m SE of High Clanyard farmhouse is the site of another tower connected with the Gordons of Clanyard.

High Drummore motte (NX 130353)

A small motte, here with a quite visible bailey. A coastal promontory is again the location; although the disfigured mound survives to only some 2.5m in height, its oval summit measuring 10m by 6.3m. The bailey to the E measures 28m by 20m within a very wide (7m+) bank. The latter evidently also enclosed the motte, until later cultivation removed a lengthy section.

Isle of Lochnaw (NW 993632)

Late 1990s surveys of this tree-covered islet in Lochnaw, 420m NE of the presently inhabited Lochnaw Castle (of 15th century and later build) have resulted in a reinterpretation of the site. The consensus remains that the earliest stone building was a vaulted hall-house, i.e. the castle captured by Archibald the Grim, Earl of Douglas, in 1390. This is now known to have measured approximately 15.5m by 10m internally, within a wall over 2m in width. However, it may not as thought have been slighted and abandoned in 1390, but vacated in 1426 and later reoccupied for an indefinite purpose in the 17th century when a new structure was built at one end. This itself was demolished, possibly when the loch was drained in the 18th century, at which time a drystane dyke was built around the perimeter. Water-filled again, Lochnaw's sequential island castle cannot normally be visited.

It has been suggested the shore promontory opposite, later named 'Sir Stair's Island', may have served as a form of bailey (or at least landing stage) to the island castle. The stone 14th century tower/hall on the castle isle may well have replaced an earlier defensive residence on the site, as with 12th century castles established on lochs at Kirkcudbright Loch Fergus, Lochrutton, and elsewhere. However a now-vanished motte is said to have stood close to the Loch, apparently dug up in road construction; though its authenticity is unverified.

Kildonan - castle site (NX 059519)

A tower-house allegedly once stood somewhere in the vicinity of the farmhouse.

Kilhilt - castle site (NX 059558)

Site of a tower-house on a low plateau N of the Garthland Burn, approximately 350m NE of Colin farmhouse.

Killaser Castle (NX 096451)

South of the c.1900 Ardwell parish church are the rubble-strewn lower portions of a tower house (approximately 6.5m by 4.8m within walls 1.5-2m thick) built by the McCullochs. Amongst the remains are indications of a vaulted ground floor, mural passage, and possibly the opening for a stair to former upper levels.

Lochnaw Castle (NW 991628)

The castle was likely begun by the Agnew's, soon after receiving a grant of the lands from Margaret, Countess of Douglas, in 1426. The initial structure comprised a tower-house, a simple rectangular with machicolated parapet, and probably an ancillary barmkin wall, later replaced in subsequent phases of addition and rebuilding. The small 15th century tower measures around 7m square, and is of four storeys with a crowstepped caphouse of probable 16th construction (a gunloop below is most certainly a 16th century insertion). Ranges of buildings were added to the tower in the 17th-19th centuries, enclosing a courtyard. Unfortunately, however, two of these were demolished soon after the Second World War. The present tower-house entrance is not original, probably having been repositioned in the 18th century. For some years of late the castle served as a hotel.

Low Ardwell - castle site (NX c.082465)

Possible tower-house site; a castle is said to have been here by tradition.

Marslauch - castle site (NX 014671)

Nothing remains of a tower said to have been located in a field SW of Marslauch farm.

Stranraer St John's Castle (NX 060608)

Built c.1510 in the then village of Chappell (dedicated to St John) the tower's fortunes have recently revived following conversion to the 'Castle Museum'. Comprising an L-plan block of originally three storeys above a ground floor, a top floor was added c.1600 (original roundels and caphouse being removed in the process) and further altered in the early 19th century. These alterations reflected the ongoing use of the tower as a prison, court, and police station; though by the early 1900s it was serving as a storehouse. St John's Castle is perhaps best associated with Graham of Claverhouse, the vilified 'Bloody Clavers' of Covenanting tradition, who in the early 1680s used the castle as a base while sheriff of Wigtown. Earlier it had been the

property of the Adairs, passing to the Kennedys in 1590 (five years before the 1595 creation of Stranraer as a burgh of barony). The building interior has seen much subdivision for separate debtors and criminal cells. Ironically the original pit-prison, considered too inhumane by the Georgian era, fell into disuse.

St John's Castle (McGibbon & Ross)

Wigtownshire - East Rhins

Balneil - castle site (NX c.184639)

A former 'Manor House of the Rosses' stood on this site (a slope E of the present farmhouse) or nearby in the Glebe field. Following the Reformation the lands of Balneil (formerly owned by Glenluce Abbey) are known to have been granted by the Earl of Cassillis to Patrick Vaus of Barnbarroch, passing briefly to the Rosses the following century, then by marriage to the Dalrymples of Stair. The initial builder of Balneil and any phase(s) of rebuilding can only be conjectured. It is believed to have been abandoned for the new house at Carscreugh by c.1670.

Castle Kennedy (NX 110609)

Standing on a ridge in-between the Black and White lochs, the picturesque shell of this large 17th century mansion now forms the chief 'ornament' of outstanding Gardens first laid out by William Adam. The Kennedys began work soon after 1600, replacing an existing structure (on record as early as 1426) on-site. The grandiose new 'castle' consisted of a four-storey and garret central block flanked by towers on the E side, and turrets (one containing a stair) in the two re-entrant angles on the W. Some minor provision was made for defence by way of ground floor gunloops, one flanking the doorway in the SE re-entrant. In 1605 it was described in a charter as the *novum castrum de Inche*. An intention to extend the main block was evidently never undertaken. Shortly before the fire of 1716, towers were added to the S and W. Within, the originally vaulted ground floor contained the standard service rooms, the main block above housing public rooms and bedchambers in the towers. Following the blaze the Dalrymples of Stair (owners since 1677) removed to Culhorn, perhaps at first intending to restore Castle Kennedy. However the family did not return until the 1860s, and then to the huge baronial mansion of Lochinch -

Castle Kennedy

itself designed as the centrepiece of a new estate incorporating the old castle.

Castle of Park (NX 188571)

Large and intact L-plan tower-house of 1590-99, on a highly visible site above the Water of Luce. Later (18th century) low wings on two sides have been removed. The inscribed lintel above the gunloop-flanked doorway commemorates the first residents, Thomas Hay of Park and his wife Janet MacDowel. Four storeys, and an additional garret in the jamb, in height, a prominent feature is a massive chimney-stack rising from the wallhead. The Hays vacated the tower in the early 19th century for their recently rebuilt residence at nearby Dunragit Castle (see below). In recent decades Castle of Park has undergone consolidation and internal work, the building now being maintained by the Landmark Trust.

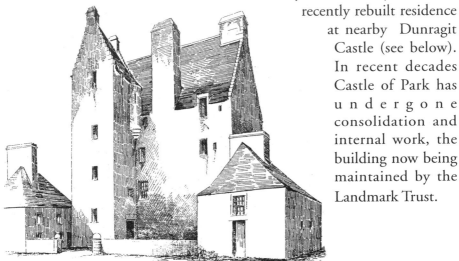

Castle of Park, before removal of low wings (McG&Ross)

Craigcaffie (NX 089641)

Happily restored and again serving as a private home, this rectangular tower-house of three storeys and a garret (with parapet on two sides) was built for John Neilson and his wife Margaret Strang in the 1570s - a fact attested by a skewputt monogram. Fine details include roundels and a bretasche (projecting machicolation) above the doorway at parapet level, continuous corbelling, and ornamental spouts; although the dormer windows are modern replacements. The tower may have replaced on-site the caput of an estate mentioned during the reign of

Craigcaffie

Robert Bruce (1306-29). However, traces of a ditch surviving until more recent centuries now seem undetectable. The Neilsons owned the lands of Craigcaffie from Bruce's time until the late 18th century, when they passed to the ascendant Earls of Stair.

Cults - possible motte site (NX 123599)

Former descriptions of a small but distinctive mound may indicate a motte. The last traces were seemingly removed during WWII construction of the Cults airfield.

Dunragit (NX 150582)

Dunragit House, an nondescript mansion of 18th-19th century build, contains at its SW angle portions of an earlier building, possibly a 16th century tower-house. The property of Dunragit was acquired by Cuthbert Bailey, the commendator of the nearby Cistercian abbey of Glenluce, around the time of the Battle of Flodden (1513). He or a successor may have built the tower now represented by the encased fragment. This property also passed to Dalrymple of Stair in the 18th century, who began building the present composite house.

Droughdool 'motte' (NX 148569)

A prominent though eroded mound, now situated in a clearing of trees south of the A75 at Dunragit, recently underwent some excavation. The results led to the assumed motte's medieval status being questioned, and a Bronze Age origin posited. There was apparently never a ditch around the mound (arguably ruling out even medieval re-use); while its sides were seemingly stepped when first constructed.

Freugh - castle site (NX 111561)

Immediately north of the airfield. A tower-house and its policies are shown on a map of 1795, but appear to have been cleared before c.1850. The lands, and possibly an early fortalice, were owned by a branch of the MacDowalls in the 15th century. In 1654 the tower was burnt, soon afterwards the laird of Freugh moving to Balgreggan.

Glenluce 'Mote Hill' (NX 194573)

Despite the traditional appellation, this disfigured earthwork on a steep and tree-covered promontory (at the W end of Glenluce village) may have originated (and seen sole use as) a pre-medieval centre of local lordship. Traces of two ramparts survive, behind which the defended area measures around 90m by 50m.

Inch Crindil (NX 104408)

A possible residence of the Bishops of Galloway, supposedly sited on an island in the White Loch near Castle Kennedy. 'The Manor Place of Inch' is recorded in the 15th and 16th centuries; although a survey of the site in the 1960s observed no visible remains. During the Kennedy occupation of the 17th century mansion, the Earl of Cassillis boated to a 'little house' on the Inch for periods of rest.

Innermessan motte (NX 084633)

A large motte of regular form, with a summit approximately 30m in diameter. On one side the ground drops steeply to a beach below, enabling clear visibility over Loch Ryan. A ditch around 11m wide (but now only 1m deep) and a stream together enclose the landward approaches, while traces of trenches may represent an 19th century excavation by antiquarians. The present earthwork could well overlie or be adjacent to an earlier centre of lordship (one revisionist interpretation of 'Rheged' suggests Innermessan as a principal centre). Given the strategic location of Innermessan, especially in considering the importance of war galleys (and water transport in general) in the Irish Sea during the medieval era, one might conjecture Innermessan as representing a motte erected by Gilbert before the post-1185 infeudation of Wigtownshire. Just as likely, it is representative of the latter process.

Larg Castle - site of (NX 166642)

Site of a tower possibly constructed by John Vaus of Longcastle and Barnbarroch, who received the Larg property formerly held by Soulseat Abbey at the Reformation. In the 17th century Larg went to the family of Lynn. Mains of Larg steading may well stand on the tower site.

Old Halls of Craig - site of (172598)

Like the afore-mentioned Larg, this site around 2 miles S was probably a modest tower-house, quite possibly built on former Church lands following the Reformation. Traces of a later steading remain.

Round Dounan (NX 148579)

A possible motte, and if so then one fashioned from a natural knoll, lying within woods SW of Dunragit House. The close proximity of Droughdool motte need not in itself rule out the possibility of another caput of feudal lordship (the situation, representing a subordinate fief, occurred elsewhere); although Round Dounan may well represent another earlier (native) centre of lordship. An irregular surface area measures approximately 28m by 25m, placing it almost in the homestead-motte category. A wide platform flanks the base of the mound on its W side.

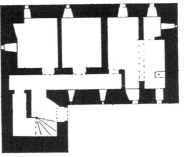

Castle of Park, plan of ground-floor; (left) doorway, with flanking shothole, and inscribed lintel and armorial panel above

Wigtownshire - Machars and Penninghame

Auchenmalg (NX 237521)

In a field above the bay, and clearly visible from the shore road, is a fragment of a tower built by the Adairs.

Baldoon Castle (NX 425537)

Baldoon

On one side of the now partly overgrown WWII airfield, and famed for its setting for Sir Walter Scott's *The Bride of Lammermoor*, stands an ivy-covered fragment of the Scott's probable c.1600 tower or early mansion. Less survives today than at the mid-19th century date of the drawing shown. Fronting the remains, however, are a pair of ornate 17th century gate-piers. In the immediate vicinity is a later farmhouse and steading.

Barmeal Castle - site (NX 378413)

East of Monreith, on a rocky bluff on the N side of the A747, is the site of a tower-house now represented by only a stretch of (barmkin?) wall incorporated in a later dyke, and some scattered rubble.

Boreland of Clugston motte (NX 355584)

East of Kirkcowan is another seemingly undocumented motte, again without any surviving traces of a bailey. Having subsided even over the past century (the erosion ascertained from earlier surveys), the 5.5m high tree-topped mound has an oval summit measuring approximately 8m by 7m, within a ditch 6m wide and 1m deep that remains on all sides but the east.

Castle Feather (NX 448342)

A coastal promontory fort, of probable prehistoric origin, was apparently readapted as a defensive residence sometime during the medieval era. A broad wall (2m in width, and surviving to over 2m in height) was built behind the innermost of the fort's three isolating ditches, while several buildings (one a small tower-house?) within the fort are indicated by overgrown footings. There appears to be no historical documentation relating to this site.

Carscreugh (NX 223598)

Situated at the end of a farm road 2 miles NE of Glenluce, only a fragment remains of a once substantial mansion constructed c.1665x80 for James Dalrymple, 1st Earl (later Viscount, and Lord Advocate) of Stair. The nearby Balneil appears to have been abandoned for Carscreugh, which when completed formed a U-plan symmetrical mansion comprising a main

Carscreugh, as depicted in 19th century (McG&R), and (top, insert) today

block and short wings. One of the latter, with a circular stair-tower in a re-entrant, is the only surviving component. Much of the rest of the collapsed building has probably been removed for the usual purposes.

Castle Stewart motte and tower-house (NX 379960)

Lying to the W of the A714, 3 miles N of Newton Stewart, and alongside a heavily subsided motte, is the ruin of a rectangular tower-house probably dating from soon after 1500. Originally of four storeys, the S and W walls mostly remain to the level of corbels formerly supporting a wall-walk. There appears to have been no ground-floor vault, while the exterior corners have been rounded to minimise on the need for dressed stone - both cost-saving measures. Viewed from the angle between the largely collapsed N and E walls, interior features (obscured at time of writing by scaffolding) include large

Castle Stewart

first and second floor windows (the latter with chamfered jambs), wall chambers, and an ornately carved fireplace on the second floor (a portion of another is visible on the third). When built the tower was known as Culquhreauch, or Culcruchie, being renamed in the 17th century by the then owner Colonel William Stewart. In 2005-06 the ruin is in the process of consolidation; however, a recently-built house and enclosing fence prevent close inspection.

Castlewigg (NX 427432)

The ivy-clad shell of this secluded mansion incorporates an L-plan tower-house at one corner. The tower was built for Archibald Stewart of Barclye and Tonderghie, who acquired the lands in 1584 from Sir John Vaus. Visible features include a first-floor corniced window, roll-mouldings, a lintel dated 1593, and a doorway-flanking gunloop in the jamb. A partly-vaulted ground floor was later used as a wine cellar for the adjoining c.1800 house. The

Castlewigg: bow-fronted c.1800 addition (tower-house to rear)

present stair is a Georgian replacement. A fragment of doorway some 30m from the tower may represent the entrance to a former barmkin/courtyard.

Clary - Bishop's Palace site (NX 424603)

Another site in the old Penninghame locale associated with the Bishops of Galloway. A retired architect (the late Dick Ilyffe) recently residing at Clary considered an adjacent barn to contain *in situ* portions of a large 15th-16th century tower-house. The Bishops are certainly believed to have had a residence here in the late medieval period, a property eventually passing to the Earl of Galloway. Stones in a later garden wall may be connected with this building. Mary Queen of Scots possibly stayed here, or at Penninghame Hall (see below), in August 1563.

Craichlaw (NX 306611)

A tower-house built c.1500 by William Gordon, second son of John Gordon of Lochinvar. Its surviving lower portions now form the oldest section of a larger mansion of 18th-20th century build. The ground-level doorways and entire upper level date from the 1860s. Within, the original turnpike stair was replaced; while an armorial panel probably once surmounting the c.1500 entrance has been reset in the first floor hall.

Crailloch motte and tower-house site (NX 327526)

A partly artificial motte of quadrangular shape, with the form having being most likely dictated by the rocky hillock over which the structure was raised. Traces of stone around the summit edge have been deemed to represent a later wall forming a farm enclosure; however, the Dunbars had a tower-house here by the early 16th century - though whether exactly on the earlier site or not is unclear. A rock-cut ditch surrounds most of the perimeter, and it has been suggested this feature dates from the Early Historic period. Equally, Crailloch may well have been occupied through periods of early lordship until the 12th-13th century, and beyond to the Dunbars time (a common sequence, but one usually only verifiable by excavation).

Cruggleton Castle (NX 485428)

A dramatically situated promontory castle. However destruction, subsequent quarrying, and natural clifftop erosion have all contributed to the near-disappearance of this once formidable stronghold. In probability a continuous site of lordship from the Early Historic period, extensive archaeological excavation has revealed evidence of a partly artificial motte (i.e. a scarped and raised promontory head) with timber defences - most likely the work of Roland after 1185 - being in turn enclosed by an irregularly shaped stone curtain wall around a century later. The latter was almost certainly undertaken by Alexander Comyn, and involved a huge new foundation being laid around the motte base with several stone towers projecting from the curtain wall. The most sizeable of these (on what was a fairly restricted site) had dimensions of 10m by 15m. This impressive replacement castle had an entrance reached by a raisable drawbridge spanning a recut ditch. Edward Bruce (brother of King Robert) captured Cruggleton in 1308, with the customary Bruce demolition following soon after. However by the 1360s the castle had been partly reconstructed by either the priors of Whithorn (who held the wider estate) or the Douglases (who may have acquired the castle site), its principal features comprising a rebuilt gatehouse and a new tower-house erected within (and utilising the foundations of) one of the Comyn-built towers. A fragment of vault from the 1360s tower remain's, along with extensive ditches relating to both 'motte', and a huge outer enclosure only ever defended by earth and timber.

Druchtag motte (NX 349466)

Situated a quarter-mile north of the parish kirk, this well preserved motte is

Druchtag motte.view from road beneath mound

another probably originating from soon after Roland's 1185 invasion. A substantial ditch surrounds the steep-sided mound (summit diameter 20m); later filled in on the W for a road now intersecting the site. The road would also have obscured any trace of an adjoining bailey at this point; although traces of such may be indicated in the field on the west. Typically nothing is known of the presumably Anglo-French knight granted the fief of these lands; but in the later medieval period they were held by the McCullochs ('of Druchtag').

Drumgin - castle site (NX 402444)

Near Ravenstone is a scant earthwork indicative of a moated-manor.

Isle of Whithorn Castle (NX 476365)

A still inhabited and harled L-plan tower-house, rather late for the genus in dating from c.1670. A low wing projecting from the N is of 19th century construction. But otherwise the tower exterior incorporates the standard features of roundels/bartizans, crowstepped-gables, with larger windows placed at upper levels. The builder was Patrick Houston of Drummaston. Subsequent uses have included: a government base in the fight against smuggling; a butcher's shop; and a boarding house in the mid-20th century

Loch Maberry (NX 286751)

Close by the B7027, is the otherwise remotely situated Loch Maberry. Its surface is dotted by several islands, three of which appear to have been occupied during the medieval period. The largest of these (approximately 35m by 25m), is enclosed by the base of an unmortared wall, with an apparent landing place and signs of buildings within. Two other islands show traces of walling, at least one of these being apparently connected by a causeway to the main isle. Another causeway reportedly linked the latter to the shore (these were allegedly visible in former times, and may yet appear today at times of low water level). It would be feasible to suggest Early Historic occupation of the site, with the present remains possibly representing an undocumented castle (a hall and stone enclosure?) of the 13th century. The sequence is certainly witnessed elsewhere in the region.

Longcastle (NX 394469)

In addition to housing around ten former crannogs, the drained (since 1863) Dowalton Loch contains an apparently natural knoll (once an island) where the McDowalls, holders of the Barony of Longcastle in 1330, seemingly built a hall-house within a small enclosure, possibly replacing an existing structure in the process. Overgrown foundations of what appear unusually thick walls enclose a small courtyard area with traces of former buildings within. One of these, feasibly a hall, appears to have had dimensions of some 15m by 5m. A vanished medieval chapel stood on a hill nearby (Chapel Hill NX 393473).

Mindork - castle site (NX 322588)

A Dunbar tower-house described as having had a barmkin and containing much dressed stone, now consists of some scattered heaps of rubble, with presumably the cut stone having been removed in recent centuries.

Mochrum Castle Loch (NX 293541)

This island on the tellingly named Castle Loch was the location of a hall-house built by the Dunbars in the late 14th or early 15th century. There may have been an earlier defence here, the incidence being common throughout the region. Abandoned as a residence probably in the 15th century (see below: Old Place of Mochrum), the Marquis of Bute consolidated (and 'enhanced') the ruin in 1911. Accorded similar treatment by the devoutly Catholic family was an attached chapel.

Myrton tower-house and motte (NX 360432)

Within the Monreith estate is the extremely rare incidence of a tower-house having been built upon a motte-summit. Defence, and perhaps symbolism, was evidently considered still of paramount importance, as towers placed upon mottes elsewhere were wont to collapse or quickly subside (mottes being largely soil mounds, were intended only for timber structures). However a more secure foundation may well have been first dug into the motte base. The tower, later converted in part to a dovecot, is heavily overgrown with ivy; but discernible at parapet level is simple chequer-course corbelling, ornamental spouts, and angle rounds. Three gunloops survive at ground-floor level. Large first-floor windows with cornices on three surviving sides; and, within, a fragment of fireplace. A probable early 17th century wing to the N, extending beyond the motte, has been reduced to its lower levels. This structure was itself L-shaped, and has a stair turret in one re-entrant. Doors and interior features suggest an 18th century renovation. The first tower was the work of the McCullochs, undertaken sometime in the early 1500s. King James IV is known to have resided here while on a Whithorn pilgrimage in 1504. In 1683 the property was acquired by the Maxwells, who probably vacated the present ruin for a newly-built mansion - the nearby Monreith House - in the late 1790s.

Myrton Castle and motte, 19th century view (McG&Ross)

Old Place of Broughton - castle site (NX 456452)

A location where complete disappearance unusually testifies to the soaring fortunes of the owner-builders, the site of this castle is now marked by scant indications of an oval-shaped ditch. This may represent an early (12th-13th century) ringwork (scarce in Galloway, but plentiful for example in Renfrewshire) and/or the ditch for a later tower or hall-house. What is concretely known about Broughton, however, is that it was rebuilt in 1628 by the Murrays of Broughton (rivals of the nearby Hannays of Sorbie), the heraldic stone from the building having been later reset in Broughton Mains farmhouse.

By an astute marriage, Richard Murray of Broughton acquired the Cally estates, with successive generations building and augmenting the neo-classical Cally 'palace' near what became Gatehouse-of-Fleet (and marrying also into the Earl of Galloway's family). A sumptuous town-house built (or begun) c.1750 by the Murrays in Kirkcudbright assumed the name of Broughton House, with the 'Old Place' in the Machars 'back-water' being meanwhile left to tumble down and serve as local building material (a process doubtless accelerated by the construction in 1841 of a brickworks in an adjacent field).

Old Place of Mochrum (NX 308541)

Around the end of the 15th century the Dunbars apparently built a tower-house here to replace their existing residence on Mochrum Loch (see above), a structure now lying on the W side of an enlarged and heavily restored courtyard block. Towards the end of the 17th century this plain rectangular tower (9m by 7m) was augmented by a T-plan version, the two linked by a wall (possibly part of a larger barmkin). The combined structure was a ruin when it passed to the infant third Marquis of Bute in the mid-19th century. A keen (and soon famed) medievalist, in 1873 he commenced a programme of restoration continued by his son the 4th Marquis, who undertook an almost complete rebuild of the remainder in the early 1900s. Accordingly, most wallhead details (including corbelling, crowstepped gables and chimneys) date from Victorian times. The large N range and the E range are almost entirely Victorian-Edwardian, less attempt being here made in mock-medieval appearance by the 4th Marquis. The evidently wealthy Butes were fervent restorers nationwide, e.g. Mount Stuart, Cardiff Castle, and Castle Coch are all Bute commissions. Although again a rebuild, the c.1900 courtyard entrance was raised on original foundations. Descendants still own the property. Flora Stuart, Lady Bute, lived here until her death in 2005.

Old Place of Monreith (NX 381430)

Also known variably as the Old Place of Dowies, Dowies Castle, or 'the Moure' (site of an older castle, possibly a former motte, nearby at NX 382433), this tower recently restored from dereliction was built by the Maxwells around or soon after 1600. Consisting of two storeys and a garret, it is a T-shaped variation on the standard L-plan, here the wing projecting from the centre of the main block's E side. A round and conical-roofed stair

'Dowies', before removal of additions (McG&Ross)

turret and large wallhead chimney dominate the W face, the former carrying gunloops. Moulded doorway and windows of 17th century date, with some probable 18th century alterations. Above the first-floor window on the S gable is a gargoyle of two heads, most likely reset skewputts removed during recent centuries of farmhouse use. Dormer windows are 1980s replacements; likewise the doorway jambs. Members of the Maxwells of Monreith family stayed here until 1683.

Penninghame Hall - site of (NX 409605)

Traces of a ditch and stones indicating a courtyard in the vicinity of this episcopal centre probably represent a former palace of the Bishops of Whithorn.

Ravenstone Castle (NX 409441)

The 1990s saw substantial restoration of this multi-period structure from a state of dereliction, returning it to the role of private residence. The present castle comprises four main construction-stages: a late 16th century L-plan tower-house, remodelled and given an extending wing late in the following century; a northern extension of the whole and full-height double-bowed front added c.1775; and a further extension to the N added in the later 19th century.

The re-entrant and two sides of the first tower are encased in later work; however, on the surviving exterior several roll-moulded windows and a gunloop are original. The first builders were probably the Kennedys of Blairquhan; with the later 17th century work undertaken by Robert Stewart, whose grandfather (the first Earl of Galloway) came into possession of the

Ravenstone Castle

estate during the Civil War. Descendants undertook the 18th century third stage as described; Lord Borthwick who purchased the estate in 1874, the fourth. Much more recently, renovations continue under the present owner.

Sinniness Castle (NX 214531)

Ruinous portions of a tower-house built by the Kennedys, probably during the early 16th century (possibly on the site of an earlier structure). Apparently rectangular in form, it originally rose to three storeys beneath an attic. The N gabled end forms the main surviving fragment, while a ground floor evidently contained two vaulted cellars.

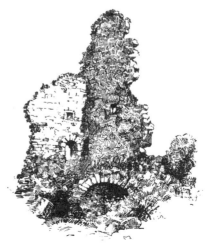

Sinniness Castle (McGibbon & Ross)

Skaith motte (NX 381662)

A tree-covered, low and almost square mound, surrounded by a ditch and bank, would appear to fall into the generic category of homestead-motte (unseen elsewhere in Wigtownshire, unless Crailloch is considered; Rispain Camp was previously suggested as a large and irregular homestead motte but has since dated to the 1st century AD). The summit of Skaith is small, some 12m by 10m; however in one corner are indications of a former building, seemingly L-shaped in plan.

Sorbie motte (NX 451469) and 'Old Place of' (NX 451471)

One of the few mottes for which documentary evidence survives - the

builders being almost certainly the Vieuxponts who received the lands from Roland in or after 1185 - stands near the substantial shell of a late 16th century L-plan tower-house. An excavation during the 1970s revealed continuous occupation of the motte through the 12th-16th centuries, until final abandonment (and subsequent landscaping) for the tower. The latter represents the work of the Hannays, and in recent times has been consolidated by the Clan Hannay Society. It appears to have been a comparatively grand undertaking for a family of only local importance; while its construction may even have resulted from attempted one-upmanship in a matter of rivalry with the nearby Murrays of Broughton. Features of note include corbelling formerly supporting bartizans at three angles; a stair-turret projecting from the re-entrant carrying a macabre carved head; a roll-moulded doorway; and, within, a restored kitchen fireplace and scale-and-platt stair to the hall. The ground floor as usual carries a vault. Typically the timbers for the upper floors have gone, making however for clear viewing of the spacious upper chambers from the first floor. Despite consolidation of the building of late it has been locked, though with information and contacts available on-site by way of an exterior display board.

Whithorn Bishop's Palace - site (NX 449404)

At Balnespik, on a location under cultivation 300m W of the priory, is another castle site associated with episcopal residence. If related to the mid-12th century revival of the Bishopric and accompanying erection of a church, it may well have been a ringwork.

Wigtown Castle (NX 438550)

Positioned beneath the medieval town on a site originally at the mouth of the Bladnoch, since an early 19th century redirection of the river this faint earthwork now lies some 200m inland. A conjectural reconstruction drawing on a nearby display board suggests the river may have filled a ditch still traceable on the castle's N side - giving it complete water defence as at Caerlaverock (and possibly Buittle). The drawing does not, however, depict a former twin-towered gatehouse, footings of which (with the dressed plinth stones removed) can be seen at the W end of the roughly oval court. Meanwhile, a large rectangular building (a hall or tower?) is indicated by a faint mound on the S side. No record of Captain McKerlie's excavation of 1830 appears to have survived, although one fears this opening up of the site may have resulted in even more quarry use (e.g. for the harbour area).

Wigtown was most likely established as a sheriffdom in or soon after 1247, with the stone castle possibly contemporary with this process. Edward I considered the coastal castle of sufficient strategic importance to assume control of it himself in 1291. Like Kirkcudbright and others, eventual destruction followed capture by forces loyal to Robert Bruce in their ravaging of the region prior to Bannockburn.

Western Kirkcudbrightshire

Anwoth/'Boreland of Anwoth' motte (NX 584550)

This interesting earthwork, an irregular motte-and-bailey, perhaps marked the western-most limit of Anglo-French infeudation prior to Roland's later (post-1185) subjugation of the territories west of the Cree. Unlike most other mottes found in Galloway, Anwoth was clearly built with a large and strongly defended bailey. In a situation commonly seen in Ulster, when erected it may have represented a 'frontier castle' before Gilbert's native-held lands in present-day Wigtownshire (see also below: Kirkclaugh). Its builder was most likely a David fitz Teri, who appears to have received a grant of surrounding land from Uchtred (and hence is dateable to 1160 or soon after). The site chosen was a long ridge projecting into the Water of Fleet estuary, this feature being scarped and the southern third (closest the sea) cut off from the rest of the summit (itself measuring around 100m long by 30m wide in its entirety) by a 15m wide ditch. Another, deeper, ditch fronted the bailey on the mainland side.

Barholm Castle (NX 520529)

On an elevated setting high above the A75, now visible for miles over Wigtown Bay, this recently restored and brightly harled tower was probably built during the early-mid 16th century by the McCullochs - although a blocked first-floor apparent doorway suggests a 15th century tower may have been later adapted and given a jamb. Nonetheless, appearing of standard four storey L-plan, at 3rd floor a stair-turret projects from corbelling in the re-entrant angle. On the exterior, of note are a segmental-arched doorway with an ornate and highly distinctive rope moulding, and an ogee-headed upper window in the jamb. A vaulted ground floor contains a cellar and aumbries. Usual arrangement of first-floor hall and bedchambers above.

Barmagachan motte (NX 613494)

A classic pudding-bowl motte, sited less than one mile from the more irregular Roberton (see below), now stands some 6m high (with summit diameter of 17m) above a burn. A ditch surrounding its base is still discernible. Recently, Barmagachan has been suggested as having been constructed by one Bernard de Ripley around c.1235.

Balmangan Castle (NX 651456)

The lowest portion of a rectangular, evidently vaulted, tower-house of probable early 16th century date now lies in a private garden.

Borgue motte/Boreland of Borgue (NX 646517)

One of the half-dozen or so Galloway mottes authentically verified by charter evidence to an incoming knight: here one Hugh de Moreville, from an important family already established in Lauderdale and north Ayrshire. The lordship of Borgue came either directly from the Crown, or indirectly by way of the newly 'feudalised' Uchtred (son of Fergus, deprived of the old Lordship of Galloway in 1160). Less impressive than de Berkeley's Motte of Urr, the actual motte at Borgue is, however, larger, but lacks Urr's huge fort-like enclosing bailey. An elevated location was chosen by de Moreville, with the actual mound being constructed over a rocky hillock, and surrounded by a ditch and counterscarp bank. The area of the summit measures approximately 35m by 25m, rising some 6-7m high above the surrounding field. A former bailey may have been ploughed out; however, a second piece of rising rocky ground to the S has been suggested as having provided the function. Around c.1200 the lordship of Borgue passed to the de Campania family, the smaller lordships thereafter accounting for Barmagachan and Roberton mottes being largely formed out of it.

Burned Island (NX 657728)

This possible former crannog (lying off the the W shore of Loch Ken) seems to have functioned as an important centre of lordship in eastern Galloway from the Dark Ages through to its role as the probable mid-13th century administrative seat of Devorgilla and John Baliol's portion of the Galloway Lordship (if giving way to Buittle in this respect). Later still, it appears to have been reoccupied by the Baliols during their 1330s-50s spell of (English-aided) resurgence. The actual defensive structure on *Insula Arsa* was probably modest; as, quite apart from the added security of a lake setting, a crannog foundation would not support a building such as the

Baliol's impressive island castle of Loch Doon. Any survey of the remains would now be hampered by the part-submergence of the Island resulting from the Loch water-level having being raised in the 1930s.

Cally motte (NX 606556)
Lying within Girthon parish (1.5 miles N of Girthon Old Parish Church), now in the policies of Cally House ('Cally Palace Hotel') stands a medium-sized motte beside a burn. It remains to some 5m high, has a summit (its surface obscured by trees) approximately 25m in diameter, and is surrounded by a ditch. There are no obvious signs of an attached bailey. By the end of the 13th century the lands of Girthon were in possession of the de la Zouch family.

Cardoness Castle (NX 590522)
Well-preserved and maintained by Historic Scotland, the shell of this late 15th century rectangular tower-house stands on a rocky bluff above the Water of Fleet. The site was originally a promontory jutting into the estuary

Cardoness Castle, 19th century view (Harper)

itself, until the latter was canalised in the 19th century. Hence it was a position of some strength and importance, and a noted place of strength in the Anglo-Scottish wars of the 1540s. The builders of Cardoness were McCullochs, granted the lands centuries after a John and Michael de Cardoness were mentioned (as pro-Baliol knights) in 1296. Their caput may in fact have been the motte at Anwoth - and less likely the site of the tower itself. Keyhole gunloops on three ground-floor sides are indicative pre-c.1520 type. Turnpike stair in wall thickness at one corner; at entresol level, this gives entry to a small prison room, with a grimmer pit-prison below. A murder-hole (doubling as goods hatch - doubtless a more usual use) is located above the inner doorway. The first-floor hall above the vaulted basement has a large and impressive fireplace, its mouldings surviving in part. Domestic quarters, as usual placed above, again have moulded fireplaces. Large windows with stone benches on first-floor and above. A now ruined attic was formerly contained within a wallwalk (apparently plain and without corbelling).

Carsluith Castle (NX 494541)

A roofless but otherwise complete shell of a 16th century L-plan tower-house, lies immediately S of the A75. One architectural assessment has dated the entire tower to the 1560s, and certainly the date (156-) is carried on a weathered armorial panel above the jamb doorway. A more standard interpretation however (and that given by Historic Scotland), posits an early-16th century oblong tower with the jamb added at the time indicated on the panel. Clearly there are signs of the jamb/wing being joined; yet this may merely represent haphazard technique, while the masonry appears continuous. A circular stair-turret projecting from second-floor at the join (W front) may seem to suggest one period of overall construction. There is clearly no dispute that the low wings projecting from the tower are much later, dating from an era when Carsluith served as a farmhouse complex. On the tower exterior, roundels carried on corbelling protrude from three corners. Corbelling with water spouts survives along the wallhead on the W front (gabled attic within); although the parapet above has now gone; gunloops at ground level, second floor, and in jamb caphouse. Within, the standard vaulted ground-floor contains two cellars lit by slits and gunloops, the turnpike in the jamb leading to upper levels. A first-floor hall contains a large fireplace (note salt box) and windows set within embrasures. Upper levels feature the usual fireplaces, garderobes, and aumbries. Fireplace in caphouse. In the late 1500s the Browns of Carsluith were involved in occasionally violent disputes with the McCullochs of nearby Barholm Castle.

Cassencarie (NX 476576)

Now forming the (disused) centrepiece and backdrop of a modern holiday park named - to the annoyance of traditionalists - 'Castle Cary' - this derelict four-storey rectangular tower-house was built for the Muirs of Cassencarie

in the later 16th century. The mis-matching corner turrets and crowstepped gables represent a 19th century rebuilding in the 'castellated' style. By this era a tall wing had already been added on the N side (late 18th century). Doorway in angle of two buildings, and wing to rear, also appear to be late Victorian work.

Cumstoun Castle (NX 682532)

In close proximity to its successor - the 19th century Cumstoun House - is a badly ruined rectangular tower-house of probable late 15th century build. With dimensions approximately 10m by 6.5m, the ground floor appears to have been unvaulted. Overgrown remains of a former possible barmkin surround the tower. The builders were most likely Kennedys; though the property later passed to the MacLellans, then the Dunbars. The tower may have had a medieval predecessor at the nearby earthwork of Castle Hill (NX 684534).

Dundeugh Castle (NX 602880)

Overgrown vestiges of two buildings may represent a tower-house and ancillary barmkin structure.

Garlies Castle (NX 422691)

Lower portions of a remotely situated tower-house built for the Stewarts of Garlies, who would later become Earls of Galloway. On the basis of its dimensions and vaulted ground-floor plan, when complete Garlies probably resembled strongly the slightly earlier and extant Cardoness (above), being similar also to the contemporary Rusco (below).

On the shorter (9m) N side, a doorway with gunloop alongside gives entrance to a lobby running E-W, itself with a turnpike stair (only the base remaining) and windowless guardroom at either end respectively. Two formerly vaulted cellars lit by slit windows lead off this passage, the larger of these having served as a store. An ornate fireplace with late Gothic details - presumably once housed at first-floor level or above - has been reset on the surviving lower E wall; while the remaining tall fragments of wall have clearly been stabilised in more recent times. These alterations date from a late-19th century consolidation of the ruins. In the building's SE corner there has been a pit-prison, a similar feature appearing at Cardoness and Rusco. From the overgrown footings in the vicinity, the tower-house was clearly once served by a series of ancillary buildings within a walled courtyard, somewhat larger than the usual barmkin.

Kenmure Castle, courtyard block

Kenmure Castle (NX 635764)

Dramatically sited above the head of Loch Ken (the effect somewhat reduced by trees obscuring the castle for most of the year) the shell of this substantial structure incorporates work from the 17th to the 20th century - something not instantly apparent due to the building's complete render of harl. The natural hill on which the castle stands could have been the location for an earlier residence, and though the snaking driveway cut into the hill is probably dateable to the early 19th century, the mound may well have been scarped during the late 12th or 13th century. At some point in the later-medieval period, the Gordons of Kenmure built a tower-house here. This was depicted on engravings of c.1790 which showed it comprising three-storeys and gabled attic, with bartizans protruding on continuous corbelling. The building was by then in ruins, while the drawing also depicted a courtyard wall. When reconstruction began in the early 19th century, the

Kenmure Castle, approach view from base of mound

16th century tower appears to have been demolished but a three-storey W wing of c.1630 and other portions retained. This W wing formed part of an intended courtyard block (a N side was never built), possibly began after Sir John Gordon of Lochinvar became first Viscount Kenmure in 1633.

The E-facing side of the W wing has a projecting stair-tower at its N end, decorated with rope-mouldings which extend across the entire range. Its door and panel above are each likewise framed by a rope moulding in an ogee-shaped arch. The N face of the tower (and of the entire W wing) has clearly been blocked by an Edwardian addition (with mock crenelated parapet, the interior however instantly reveals its construction of house-brick). At the re-entrant angle with the 18th-19th century S range, is another stair-tower, octagonal in shape, and possibly later 17th century. Towards the end of the 19th century an attempt was made to restyle the S end of the W wing in the image of the former tower-house (it was, after all, the era of Scots Baronial); the most distinctive feature of this being the large angle turret. Other additions are of 19th-20th century date. The interior of the castle above first-floor level is a shell. Below, features include vaulted cellars in the W wing, their gunloops altered to form small rectangular openings on the exterior. At time of writing (2006) entry within this unstable building is inadvisable. On two sides the castle is surrounded by overgrown, practically vanished gardens. A likewise overgrown tree-lined approach (and ice-house) adds to a list attesting to former grandeur. Kenmure was gutted by fire around 1950, and has lain derelict since.

Kirkclaugh motte (NX 534521)

Another coastal motte-and-bailey in Anwoth parish, even closer to the Cree than the above-described and larger Boreland, the form is again somewhat irregular. Precipitous cliffs provide obvious protection on the S side, with an L-shaped bailey shielding the roughly square motte (itself measuring 19m by 17m, and standing to around 3m in height) on the N and W. A ditch is traceable on the bailey's N front, and continues around the E side of the site. Unfortunately, bushes now obscure most of the earthwork; but there appear to be stone foundations within the bailey. The castle has been suggested as an Episcopal defence, but this seems unlikely. It may possibly even represent a sub-fief by fitz Teri to a lesser knight.

Larg Tower (NX 433663)

A late 18th century antiquarian print depicts this tower-house, an apparently rectangular structure of possible late-15th century build, as a substantial ruin. Today, however, only one corner portion stands to any height, and that just 2.5m. Traces of barmkin wall. The McKies held the lands of Larg in the 14th century.

Little Duchrae 'motte' (NX 663695)

A possible motte near the Banks of Dee, comparable in type and situation to Pulcree - here the mound being slightly curved with a diameter of around 31m. Also like Pulcree (and several others) there is documentary evidence of occupation as late as the mid-15th century, probably in the form of a timber hall and palisade. The earthwork itself may again be of 13th or early 14th century origin.

Minnigaff motte (NX 410664)

Immediately S of the 19th century parish church and graveyard (containing the 17th century kirk shell - on a still older medieval site) is the location of a castle likely that described by Blind Harry as the 'strength on the Water of Cree' captured by William Wallace in the late 1290s. An apparent motte scarped from a natural promontory at the confluence of the Cree and the Penkiln Burn, its sub-oval summit (measuring approximately 33m by 13m) is now covered by trees. Steep sides drop to the S, W and E; although the positioning of a winding road has reduced its former effect. The level N approach (through a modern extension to the graveyard) has been cut off by a 15m wide ditch, now greatly in-filled. Overgrown foundations of a bank around the summit perimeter may indicate a former stone (or earth-and-boulder) wall. The positioning of the castle and its location immediately alongside the possibly older church suggest its origin as a c.1185 fief, perhaps granted by Roland to an incoming knight.

Old Risk (NX 448701)

In woods 3 miles NE of Minnigaff, on the left bank of the Penkiln Burn, is the base of what appears to have been a small tower-house.

Palace Yard (NX 614543)

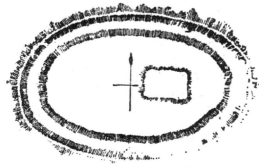

Palace Yard: 19th century plan (Harper)

Near Enrick Farm, in a low-lying field close to the modern (re-routed) A75, lies the somewhat enigmatic earthwork of 'Palace Yard'. Consisting of an oval ditch and bank enclosing an extensive area measuring 110m by 60m transversely. There are overgrown footings of what may have been a large hall-house towards the E end of the enclosure. Suggestions regarding the origin of Enrick include a possible Episcopal residence, and a 'campaign castle' of Edward I. Although, without archaeological investigation, the site fits more conveniently into the general category of 'moated-manor' - complexes of typical early-mid 14th century construction. Equally, it could be a c.1200 oval ringwork with later hall added.

Plunton Castle and ringwork (NX 605507)

An interesting incidence of a 16th century tower-house placed within a defensive oval-shaped ditch and bank of likely 12th-13th century origin. Falling possibly into the generic class of ringwork, the earthwork could represent the local caput of the de Campania family. Edward I of England ('Hammer of the Scots') may even have stayed here while in Galloway during April-May 1297. The site was quite likely in continuous occupation when the existing tower replaced a (stone or timber?) predecessor. Of L-plan with a turnpike formerly rising the full-height of the jamb, much of the interior

Plunton (note stones indicating former barmkin)

(including the stairway) has collapsed over the level of a twin-vaulted basement. Fireplaces remain on the first and upper floors, as partly do corner turrets (bartizans) formerly entered from an attic. Simple gunloops on ground-floor.

Pulcree 'motte' (NX 593583)

A possible motte, if so probably representing Anglo-French infeudation. There is, however, the usual lack of documentary evidence relating to this site, while the form of Pulcree is far from typical. This raises the possibility it may either be a native site dating from the Fergus era (or earlier), or variation of a 13th century homestead-motte. Of rectangular shape, its summit measures approximately 20m square, with a surrounding ditch on three sides and a bank dropping steeply to the Water of Fleet on the fourth. There appears to have been no bailey. Records support continued occupation until the 15th century.

Roberton motte (NX 603485)

Beside the Pulwhirrin Burn, a short distance N of Kirkandrews churchyard (the site of medieval and older finds) is another defensive earthwork, probably a motte scarped from a natural feature (and another instance of an eminence overlooking a burn). Its oblong summit measures some 27m by 14m, the mound standing to around 6m in height. A wide ditch, in part cut through solid rock, surrounds the landward approach. On the SW side are indications of a possible bailey, or perhaps just defensive bank. Roberton may have been built by Robert de Campania, nephew of Ralph de Campania who in the early 13th century succeeded the de Morevilles as lord of Borgue. This interpretation would date the motte at c.1240 - late according to traditional castle-chronology; although in northern Scotland mottes are now known to have appeared as late as the early 1300s.

Rusco Castle (NX 584604)

Another recently restored tower-house, the c.1500 Rusco resembles in plan the stump surviving at Garlies Castle and the larger (and nearer) shell of Cardoness. As noted above, the smaller two may indeed have been based on the McCulloch stronghold, the architect possibly even the same individual. Rusco was possibly built for Robert Gordon, who received the lands as dowry on marrying Mariota Carson (or 'Arcarsane'). In form the tower comprises a rectangle of three-storeys and an attic, with a vaulted ground floor containing two storerooms and an opening to the turnpike stair (here contained in the SE corner). A pit-prison arrangement is similar to the other towers mentioned. Having been returned to its original use as a private residence, the (usually vanished) timber upper floors have been replaced, and the single floor chambers partitioned into rooms (a standard practice in earlier times). Some of the internal stonework has of necessity been renewed; likewise much of the crowstepped attic (a 16th century addition in origin), parapet water-spouts, and window surrounds. At ground-floor level, keyhole gunloops similar to those at Cardoness and Garlies are again modern replacements; although the worn armorial panel above the doorway is clearly original. A wing added to the tower-house in the 17th century had a jamb containing a stair; though this range was later greatly reduced.

Trostrie and Culcraigie 'mottes' (NX 657574 & NX 657575)

Reached by minor roads leading off the N side of the A75 (within Twynholm

parish) is a large 'motte' consisting of a substantial rocky outcrop (13m in height) the summit of which has been divided in two by a stone wall. The precipitate-sided feature was also evidently once surrounded by a ditch up to 8m wide.

Trostrie and Culcraigie from 19th century sketch (Harper)

A considerable summit area measures approximately 35m by 18m. Tabraham considers Trostrie likely to have originated in the pre-motte era. The nearby lower earthwork of Culcragie could even represent infeudation, with the by-then unoccupied Trostrie serving as an additional potential strongpoint in case of attack.

Twynholm motte (NX 663542)

On the edge of the village and overlooking the Kirk Burn, lies a motte surrounded by buildings and evidently damaged by modern construction. The summit - which was previously used as small pet cemetery - measures some 13m in diameter, the motte standing to around 4.5-5m in height. A fitz Gamel of Twynholm appears on record during the early 13th century. The nearby parish church, medieval in origin, is a rebuild of c.1820.

Eastern Kirkcudbrightshire

Abbot's Tower (NX 972666)

On Landis farm, and erroneously attributed to an abbot of the nearby Cistercian foundation of New Abbey (Sweetheart), is a 16th century L-plan tower-house recently restored from a ruin. Prior to reconstruction, the only substantial portion was the W side. A new turnpike was placed in the jamb to first-floor level; here, and in the upper stories, several original features remain in the form of fireplaces, aumbries and a garderobe. Most of the rest, including the wallhead detailing and stair-tower in the re-entrant, are modern but of authentic design.

Auchenfranco Castle (NX 892724)

Close to Lochrutton is an earthwork, best described as a homestead-motte and consisting of a ditch enclosing an area measuring approximately 35m by 27m. It may have been successor to the late 12th century caput built on the loch crannog site. Nearby is the conspicuously-named Mains (from the Latin *demesne*) of Auchenfranco farm.

Auchenskeoch Castle (NX 917588)

Only a portion, in the form a circular corner-tower and one section of wall, survives from a tower-house built by the Lindsays in the later 16th century. It was apparently constructed in an in-vogue - but scarcely seen in Galloway - Z-plan style, represented today for example at Claypotts (Dundee), Drochil (Lanarkshire) and Muness (Shetland).

Auchlane Castle (NX 741584)

A MacLellan castle (possibly 14th century in origin) built on a strong site now consists of overgrown foundations, possibly representing a tower-house and barmkin. A ditch described in 1891 has almost disappeared.

Balmaclellan motte (NX 653793)

On a steep hill overlooking the kirk and village, is a motte some 10m in summit diameter and 7m in height above a ditch. Again undocumented,

Balmaclellan motte, view from kirkyard

Balmaclellan was however probably one of a grouping of knight-service fiefs along with neighbouring St John's Town of Dalry and Parton (see entries respectively). If so, the obvious placename derived from MacLellan would postdate the period of construction - but perhaps indicate lordship by the later 13th century. The summit of the motte was excavated after a fashion in the early 19th century, though no record of any findings survives.

Barclosh Castle (NX 855625)
Off a minor road beside the farm, one high portion of a former thin-walled tower-house of c.1600 date is now incorporated in a field wall.

Barscobe Castle (NX 659806)
At the bottom of a farm road north of Balmaclellan, lies this late (dated 1648) tower-house of L-plan design built by William MacLellan, son-in-law of Robert Gordon of Lochinvar. His initials, along with those of his wife (WM and MG - the G clearly representing a Gordon), appear with their coats of arms in a panel above a roll-moulded doorway. Other features include a tall wallhead chimney and pedimented dormer windows (one

Barscobe

again bearing the initials and a 1648 date). The slightly lower jamb contains a turnpike; while a small wing, lower still, to the N is of 19th century date. During this period of later use several windows were altered and repositioned. In the 1970s-80s Barscobe was restored from dereliction to re-use as a private home. Within, the tower is unvaulted.

Bombie Castle (NX 715505)

Around 3 miles E of Kirkcudbright, on a steep-sided promontory above the Gribdae Burn, is the site of another castle associated with the MacLellans. The landward (western) approach has been guarded by a ditch and bank, now disfigured by later farming work. Inside the ditch, the 'summit' (though the interior is not raised, leading to Bombie's classification as a ringwork) measures some 27m by 15m. See also below: Clownstane.

Buittle Castle (NX 819616) and 'Buittle Place' (NX 817617)

On the W bank of the River Urr, two miles downstream from the impressive Motte of Urr, lies the site of a formerly large and important 13th century courtyard castle, built by John Baliol and his wife Devorgilla as principal stronghold of their extensive lands in eastern Galloway. Recent archaeological excavations found evidence of occupation at the site from the Early Historic and even Neolithic periods; although the mid-later 13th century stone castle may have been immediately preceded by a (late 12th century?) motte, perhaps lowered for the purpose. Fragments of the stone castle remain, notably lower portions of a twin-towered gatehouse evidently once faced with ashlar and fronted by a drawbridge pit. A heavily overgrown rubble wall-course and mounds represent a curtain and demolished towers formerly lining the perimeter of an inner-ward - itself the suggested motte sited within (and protected by) a loop in the river. This inner area measures approximately 40m in diameter, having a ditch cut across its landward approach. The ditch was crossed by a raisable drawbridge, and may even have been once water-filled from the Urr.

A large outer court measures almost two acres; it being within this area that excavations took place. One of the discoveries were foundations of a possible hall-house, believed to have been built by the Baliols in the mid-14th century. By this period the earlier courtyard castle had been destroyed by forces of Robert Bruce sometime before Bannockburn (1314), the lands and ruined castle having been granted to Bruce's nephew James Douglas, but re-occupied by Edward Baliol during the brief revival of Baliol fortunes (supported locally, they were however ultimately dependent on English backing). Also revealed by the excavations: despite the perimeter of the outer ward having been defended by only a palisade and timber towers, a weak point of these defences on the N side (immediately overlooked by high ground) had been given a substantial stone (or stone and earthen) wall with a stepped plinth.

A few hundred metres W of the slighted castle, situated next to the approach road, is a harled and inhabited L-plan tower-house of two-stage 16th century build. Known as Place of Buittle, its upper storey has been truncated, with only stumps of

Buittle Place

roundels and corbelling remaining; while the present doorway dates from the 18th century (an original first-floor entrance was later blocked). The original builder of the tower appears to have been a Maxwell; but before long the property had passed to the Gordons of Lochinvar (who added the jamb and rebuilt the upper-storey c.1600). In more recent times the tower became a farmhouse, losing much of its original detail in subsequent transformation to a purely functional home.

Castlehill of Barcloy (Hestan Island in left background)

Castlehill of Barcloy (NX 854524)

A bold promontory on the coast at the mouth of the Urr estuary was utilised as a fort in Early Historic times. A rock-cut ditch and bank probably represent this period of occupation, as might the base of a large wall behind the ditch. Within the site, there are footings of what seems to have been a tower-house of indefinite date. Timothy Pont listed Castlehill of Barcloy as a residence in c.1600.

Clownstane moated-manor (NX 708501)

Near the above-described site of Bombie Castle, is an apparent moated-manor site, perhaps better described as a homestead moat, and best preserved on its NW side The standard early-mid 14th century date for the type has again been suggested here. A small excavation was conducted in 1947.

Collochan Castle (NX 920754)

A possible motte, or earlier ('native') defensive site of indefinite date, consisting of a promontory overlooking the Cargen Water which has been cut off by a trench. Within, foundations of a possible tower-house have been noted. However, more recently the site has been engulfed by forestry plantation.

Colvend ('Boreland of') motte (NX 869541)

North of the tellingly-named Boreland farmhouse is a much eroded but probable motte. It is believed that by c.1160 (or even before, when Radulf was overlord of Nithsdale) Colvend was held by one Gospatrick fitz Orm (a probable Anglo-French knight from Cumbria), who seemingly gave the lands of Southwick to his son Gilbert.

Corra Castle (NX 867661)

On the N side of the A711 4 miles N of Dalbeattie, and now incorporated in a later farm building, are the remains of a what was probably a laird's house of the early 1600s, a simple rectangle in plan.

Culdoach (NX 706537)

A probable though small motte overlooks a glen near Culdoach farm. It stands to less than 3m high, with a summit measuring 27m by 15m. Traces of surrounding ditch, most evident on the NW.

Dalry - St John's Town of, motte (NX 618813)

The largest of the above-mentioned Glenkens three-motte grouping, this artificial mound rises from a natural eminence overlooking the River Ken (and is again adjacent to the kirk). Largely obscured by village buildings on two sides, it is best seen from across the river (a recent suspension footbridge facilitating in this respect), or from the road a short distance north. The Southern Upland Way passing alongside has resulted in an information board. At this point the 10m high sides of the artificial mound can be scaled to a large summit, some 30-35m in diameter.

Drumcoltran Castle (NX 869682)

A Historic Scotland property, and another tower to have been pressed into farm use (like Carsluith, Dowies, etc, probably the main factor to have ensured near-intact survival) in the early-modern era. Drumcoltran is an L-plan tower of 16th century date; and like Carsluith, there appears uncertainty whether the jamb represents a slightly later addition to the main block (e.g. c.1550+c.1570?). Drumcoltran, however, is exceedingly plain - perhaps reflecting the Calvinistic austerity of builders whose (Latin) panel above the doorway translates: 'Keep hidden what is secret; speak little; be truthful; avoid wine; remember death; be pitiful'. The main corners are moreover slightly rounded, a measure taken to minimise the need for expensive dressed stone. The tower was in near-continuous use during the Georgian and Victorian era, resulting in much interior rebuilding, window enlargement, etc. However, a simple parapet carried on crude single corbels is largely original; so too is an attic within. The lands of Drumcoltran passed from Lord Herries to the Maxwells in 1550, a minor branch of the latter (possibly Edward Maxwell, of the Maxwells of Hills) probably building the tower. The Irvings took possession of the lands in 1668, holding them until 1799. An attached farmhouse most likely built by them has had its upper storey recently removed.

Dunrod moated-manor (NX 699459)

An earthwork in the loose category assigned others like Palace Yard, etc. Here the site lies alongside that of a former parish church (later included within Kirkcudbright parish) and 'lost' medieval village. A survey and partial excavation in 1964-65 revealed fragments of pottery from the 13th century, and later from the 15th-16th centuries, suggesting continuous occupation or at least re-occupation. The ditch around the site was apparently filled

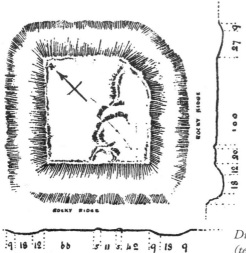

with water from the adjacent burn; while there were also traces of a stone wall around the perimeter of the earthwork enclosing a court measuring approximately 38m by 34m.

Dunrod: 19th century antiquarian sketch (terming it a "Roman" Camp)

Earlstoun Castle (NX 612840)

In a secluded position north of St John's Town of Dalry, this intact L-plan tower-house of c.1600 was built by the Gordons (whose lands and 'fortalice' of Earlstoun are mentioned in 1601) and augmented in the mid-17th century with a now-removed wing on its E side. There appear to have been no gunloops, a feature still seen elsewhere in this late phase of tower-house design (e.g. nearby at the Gordons later W wing of Kenmure); although the

Earlstoun, 19th c. sketch (MacGibbon & Ross)

vulnerable ground-floor windows are small. Large first-floor windows exhibit roll-mouldings. In the tower's S wall, a stone, presumably reset from the former c.1650 block, has the date 1655 and initials WG and MH (a similar feature having appeared several years earlier at Barscobe). The jamb of the L as usual contains a turnpike stair at the lower level, continuing from first-floor level in a turret contained in the re-entrant. Within, late 17th century panelling. A low range to the S of the tower is of 19th century date.

Edingham Castle (NX 840627) and motte site (NX 843627)

West of the A711 just north of Dalbeattie, are lower portions of a low rectangular tower-house, or plain laird's house. It has been vaulted, with a turnpike-stair evidently provided in the NW corner. A possible motte, described in the Victorian era, was later overlain by a factory.

Edingham, print from woodcut (McKerlie)

Fortalice of Greenlaw (NX 741635)

Once virtually an island within the Dee marshes, the 'fortalice' was probably a defended medieval manor or grange. A visible ditch encloses an oval area, measured at 134m by 94m. The main phase of occupation probably preceded the building of down-river Threave Castle, its defences (apart from those provided by location) almost certainly being limited to earth and timber. Land improvement in more recent centuries, resulting in the building of levees, etc., belie the former isolation. A causeway entered the fortalice from the NE. There are no indications of inner buildings, which were almost certainly only of wood.

Fourmerkland Tower (NX 909808)

A small and late (dated c.1590) rectangular tower-house, built seemingly by one Robert Maxwell, lies N of Newbridge village. Some restoration work

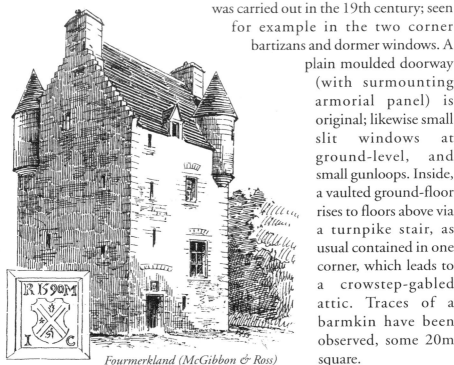

Fourmerkland (McGibbon & Ross)

was carried out in the 19th century; seen for example in the two corner bartizans and dormer windows. A plain moulded doorway (with surmounting armorial panel) is original; likewise small slit windows at ground-level, and small gunloops. Inside, a vaulted ground-floor rises to floors above via a turnpike stair, as usual contained in one corner, which leads to a crowstep-gabled attic. Traces of a barmkin have been observed, some 20m square.

Gelston - 'Boreland of'/'The Ditch' (NX 783572)

An apparent homestead-motte (or 'manor'), considered with most others in the category to post-date c.1300. However, not least in Gelston's case, this is conjecture, but without excavation all that can be said given the typical absence of documentation.

Hestan Island (NX 858303)

An island in Auchencairn Bay only accessible at low tide, was chosen by Edward Baliol as the site for a defensive residence in the 1330s. Apart from security considerations, direct access (supply and/or 'escape') by boat to the Cumbrian coast during the perilous years of short-lived Baliol revival may reflect the choice of location. The same option would be impossible or at least unfeasible from Baliol castles at Loch Doon, Burned Island, and Buittle. The castle on Hestan is now represented by footings of a rubble-built hall-house with rounded corners (perhaps yet another example of dispensing with the need for expensive dressed stone) measuring some 13m by 6.5m. The walls of the structure were fairly thin, while the doorway was in the N wall. Around the building are traces of a circular ditch, once doubtless with a palisade on its inner side. Following the Baliols' final flight in the mid-century, the castle was probably never re-occupied. Some of its stone may have gone to the construction of a nearby 19th century house.

Hills Castle (NX 912726)

Situated 1 mile S of Lochfoot village, on a site possibly once housing a 12th-13th century homestead motte, this extant and inhabited castle comprises a rectangular tower-house of c.1530, with - uniquely for the region - a complete barmkin wall, if one largely rebuilt (though containing an original gateway). In 1528 the lands of Hills were purchased from the Drumlanrig Douglases by Edward Maxwell (formerly a tenant at Breconside), who probably erected the tower soon after. His initials, along with those of his wife (Janet Carson), appear with family crests high above the tower entrance. Within, the tower has the customary vaulted ground floor and a turnpike stair in one corner; while three floors above are each of one chamber. At wallhead level: a crowstep-gabled attic entirely within a crenelated parapet; protruding ornamental cannon (drainage) spouts; continuous corbelling; and a caphouse and large chimney stack. The small but ornate two-storey gatehouse indicates a once standard barmkin feature. It formerly bore the date 1598, indicating the work of another Edward Maxwell, grandson of the above. The long wing on the tower's E side dates from the early 18th century; although it contains some reset armorial panels from an earlier wing, or from the tower itself.

Ingleston motte (NX 981651)

Near New Abbey. Sharing the name - clearly indicating Anglo-French infeudation - with a number of other mottes, the knight here can be identified as one Richard fitz Troite, an incomer from Cumbria (though probably of French descent), granted the lands of Lochkindeloch by Uchtred around 1170. The motte, now much eroded and covered by bushes and protruding rock, has evidently been built over a natural hillock. Standing to some 4.5m in height above a virtually disappeared (filled-in?) ditch, an oval summit measures approximately 26m by 15.5m.

Ingleston motte (NX 774579)

South of Gelston hamlet lies an eroded motte, the subject of intensive archaeological excavation in recent years. The mound has again been constructed over a natural rocky feature, and remains to some 5m in height with an oval summit approximately 21m by 13m. The excavations uncovered evidence of timber buildings and defences including two towers. These had apparently suffered destruction, perhaps during the rebellion of 1174. Interestingly, there appeared to have been a phase of occupation at the site pre-dating the accepted era of Anglo-French infeudation - raising (not for the first time) the question of earlier 'Norman' incomers; or even a native lord building his own 'copycat' motte (perhaps based on examples seen in nearby Cumbria). An apparent third phase of occupation may have seen the castle serve as the caput of William de Gevelstone, a knight settled in the district by Alan, Lord of Galloway, in the early 13th century. There are no signs of any former bailey, nor even a ditch.

Kirkconnell House (NX 979680)

Around 1.5 miles N of New Abbey lies another inhabited mansion house with a Maxwell-built tower at its core. The tower-house was constructed around the mid-15th century, its builder one Aymer de Maxwell who had married the heiress Janet de Kirkconnell. At some point during the following century, this rectangular structure was heightened and given a jamb to form the requisite L-plan; with, additionally, the door

being repositioned in the jamb and an attic added. A separate two-storey block was built to the N around 1660, itself added to, and the 'gap' between it and the tower filled in. Still another block was added in the 18th century; while a final extension dates from c.1820. The 15th-16th century tower-house has its original entrance on the E side now blocked, and moulded 16th century windows blocked elsewhere; gunloops likewise blocked or altered. The wallhead of the tower-house is carried on continuous and individual corbelling, and features drainage spouts. The continuous corbelling carries around the jamb, from which an additional stair leads to a crowstep-gabled caphouse.

Kirkcormack (NX 716574)

On the River Dee beside the ruin of old Kirkcormack kirk - and moreover fascinatingly medieval village site (revealed by aerial photography) - is a subsided motte, still some 5m in height and with a summit 20m by 17m. A formerly surrounding ditch has been partly filled-in. Like Gelston, the medieval Kirkcormack parish was later included in Kelton.

Kirkcudbright : Castledykes' (NX 677508)

Beside the River Dee (and now also, sewage-works), to the west of the town, are overgrown foundations of a stone courtyard castle of probable mid-later 13th century date. Once presumed to have been built by Edward I as a strategic campaign castle and garrison outpost, it is however most likely of Scottish royal build. There was almost certainly a castle here from the later 12th century, perhaps a motte (in addition to 'Moat Brae'?) later lowered for the construction of a stone curtain wall and towers. Kirkcudbright itself had been the principal power-base of Lord Fergus of Galloway before 1160. His below-described residence of 'Palace Isle' was sited on a loch north of the town. He is also credited with having built a motte to guard the town itself - probably in the years of intensifying political and military climate prior to his downfall: the vanished 'Moat Brae' (on a site which later became the friary, NX 683511).

John Comyn of Buchan was keeper of the castle when it first appears on record in 1288. In subsequent lean years of Scottish fortune (c.1296-1306), Edward I did stay at the castle (1300), and used it as a supply-base. However, as English forces and perceived collaborators were gradually expelled under Bruce, Kirkcudbright was probably taken and dismantled in the customary fashion (the use made of the castle by Edward I surely not being lost on the Scots). Detailed excavations of 1911-13 found no evidence of post early-14th century occupation, but more importantly did uncover foundations of an oblong wall of enclosure, approximately 34m by 23m, fronted by a twin-towered and buttressed gatehouse. Of two other sizeable circular towers placed at wall-angles (plus a smaller third flanking the gatehouse), one (some 13.5m in diameter) was larger, had an apparently solid base, and was presumably intended to serve as a form of keep (*donjon*). A similar layout can be seen at contemporary courtyard castles elsewhere in Scotland, e.g. Inverlochy and Coull; less so Bothwell and Direlton where clearly huge donjons provide a more obvious strongpoint and showpiece. In essence

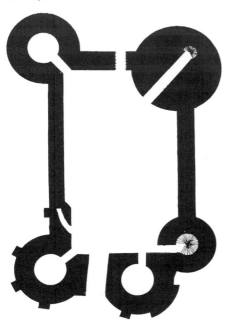

'Castledykes': post-excavation plan

the design came from French castles, especially Coucy. Like Wigtown, the castle was surrounded by a wide ditch which probably filled with water from the adjacent river. Defence apart, the importance of a coastal position for supply was here again doubtless considered of paramount importance. Traces of additional earthworks represent an outer ward, only ever defended by a ditch and palisade.

Kirkpatrick-Durham 'Moat Hill' - site (NX 795692)

Within the Georgian planned-village is a site said to have been a motte connected with the Durand family - possibly the caput of surrounding lands held by them in the 13th century.

Little Richorn (NX 835596)

Beside the River Urr, in the southern portion of the parish, is a probable moated-manor. Footings of a rubble wall were formerly (1891) reported as traceable around part of its perimeter (though such may have simply represented a farm enclosure from more recent times). On the three non-river sides there are clear indications of a wide ditch. A large area within measures approximately 45m by 52m.

Lochinvar Castle (NX 658854)

The remains of a Gordon-built castle, either a large tower or more likely a small enclosure and hall within, could be seen on an island in Lochinvar until it became submerged in 1978 (as part of a hydro-electric scheme) - a situation with obvious parallels in the cases of Loch Doon and Burned Island castles. Here, the low portions of wall surveyed in 1911 were of a structure measuring approximately 14m by 10.5m, allegedly with a circular tower formerly at one corner. The island re-emerged during a drought in 2005, but no re-survey was attempted.

Lochrinnie motte (NX 728870)

At the western-most edge of Dalry parish, this motte-and-bailey, which largely utilises a natural ridge between two burns, was previously deemed to have been of 'native' build, contemporary with or recently prior to the period of post-1160 infeudation. However, with revised notions (largely based on archaeological discovery) cautioning against strict form-based categorisation, Lochrinnie may well have originated with an Anglo-French incomer, especially given its location so far east. Regardless, the 7m high motte has a summit measuring some 30m by 14m; a lower bailey across a ditch has a smaller surface area (25m by 13m).

Lochrutton (NX 898729)

This loch seems to have been the site utilised as a caput of lordship in a similar manner to Loch Fergus - namely with two islands (again crannogs) having served effectively as a motte-and-bailey. At Lochrutton, recent carbon-dating of timber reveals the crannog to have been rebuilt c.1175X1200, while suggested documentary evidence may link this reoccupation with an incoming Anglo-French knight.

MacLellans Castle (NX 682510)

With a setting at first glance appearing somewhat incongruous, the incidence of a large tower-house having been built at the centre of an existing burgh can be explained by the background of the builder: Sir Thomas MacLellan of Bombie, Lord Provost of Kirkcudbright when the castle was first inhabited in the early 1580s. Both ambitious and holder of a genuine medieval pedigree, Sir Thomas' construction of a ground-floor containing several gunloops and a minimisation of windows (moreover capable of being barred) was at the same time practical and symbolic. Certainly, the latter was displayed in a triple heraldic panel above the door that seems to have carried the royal arms above those of Sir Thomas and his second wife (a Herries Maxwell). At the upper levels, the building was spacious and well lit by large windows, with a scale-and-platt stairway leading from ground to first floor. Elsewhere, turnpike stairs led to upper chambers (as usual now floorless) and downstairs to service rooms. A first floor hall contains an

impressive fireplace, the corner of which has a 'laird's lug' hole into a chamber behind the wall. The form of the mansion is basically L-shaped, with additional protruding blocks (in effect several jambs) and two stair-turrets projecting above ground level. Of note at parapet/eaves level: angle bartizans on two main gables; and a small section of walkway with ornamental cannon spouts for drainage. The MacLellans, like the Maxwells, were royalists during the Civil War, subsequently incurring much debt, which was not relieved by the Restoration. In the 1660s the castle was sold, stripped of its fittings, and seemingly fell into disuse. Immediately opposite is the Greyfriars church, a portion of which is an aisle of the MacLellans of Bombie. Both church and tower occupied the site of a Franciscan monastery (hence Greyfriars) cleared for the purpose. Sir Thomas probably used much of the monastery rubble for his showpiece home.

Milton Loch 'Green Island' (NX 838716)

A low promontory (approximately 75m by 22m) jutting into the loch has been cut off by a ditch and bank - possibly of medieval date. On the loch itself is a crannog (NX 839718).

Motte of Urr (NX 815647)

On the W bank of the river Urr 1 mile N of Buittle Castle, this huge and well preserved earthwork almost certainly represents a motte-and-bailey castle built by Walter de Berkeley soon after 1165. Fortunately (and rarely for Galloway) a surviving charter records the 1165 grant of surrounding lands to Walter, a knight of considerable standing and chamberlain to king William I ('The Lion') - representing the region's first period of systematic infeudation (in a process gradually moving westward). In form the castle is irregular, having its motte placed entirely within an huge bailey measuring over 150 in length by approximately 65m across. This enclosure itself has steep sides falling to a surrounding 15m wide ditch (crossed by two ramparts) with an outer counterscarp bank. At the bailey's N end, and within another ditch, a reasonably well-preserved motte mound rises another 10m high to a flat summit of approximately 25m diameter. A small-scale excavation of c.1950 found evidence of destruction (and subsequent consolidation/ rebuilding) at this level, dating this event possibly to the rebellion of 1174. The sheer scale of the bailey and its height has prompted suggestions that it may be a re-used Iron Age fort. A minor branch of the Baliols held the castle by around 1200; and while a charter was signed here in 1262, no attempt was evidently made to rebuild the fortress in stone (no small task). Archaeological finds suggest no occupation beyond the early 14th century, i.e. the principal era of Baliol demise. However, the local stand against

Bruce forces appears to have been limited to downstream Buittle, the timber-only Urr motte being quite probably abandoned.

Motte of Urr, 19th c. dramatised drawing (Harper)

Netherthird motte (NX 710554)

Another 'motte' suggested as a 'native' version, possibly post-dating the 13th century, and like others in the group almost entirely natural, here a ridge which has had two narrow ditches placed across its approachable side. Indications of stone walling are traceable around the perimeter, itself measuring some 32m by 28m. A second alternative explanation for Netherthird, is that it may have originated as a native lordship centre in the pre-feudal (or even pre-medieval) period, perhaps continuing in occupation in later centuries.

Orchardton Castle (NX 817551)

Unique in being the only round (cylindrical to be exact) tower-house in Scotland, the idea here was perhaps formed after a visit to Ireland where the form was not uncommon. The castle appears to have been built in the later 15th century, probably soon after the lands of Orchardton came into the possession of the Cairns (c.1455). The diminutive (8.5m in diameter), but happily near-complete and Historic Scotland-maintained tower, is entered by a first-floor doorway (moved from its original position) with stone forestair. The original entrance was most likely reached only by a removable timber stair; this, and a usual absence of windows (other than slits) on the ground floor, indicating that, despite Orchardton's quaint appearance, some consideration was accorded defence. A ground-floor doorway enters a vault, from where however there was no direct access above. The first-floor chamber (serving as hall) has ornamental carvings on a basin and aumbry; while all the chambers (1st-3rd floors, connected by a

Orchardton Tower, 19th century pastoral scene (Harper)

turnpike stair built within the thickness of the wall) have fireplaces and windows with stone benches. As normal, the timber floors of the upper (2nd and 3rd) levels are gone, their joist-holes evident. A corbelled (some of the corbels bearing human faces) parapet surrounds a roof of stone slabs, with a caphouse at the stair-head. The tower once had several ancillary buildings (including probably domestic accommodation) formed around a small courtyard; the foundation of these can be seen on two sides. The Maxwells of Drumcoltran obtained the property in 1633.

Palace Isle/Castle Fergus (NX 698507)

An extremely important site of major lordship in the region, is now represented by two former islands at the N end of the now-drained Loch Fergus, 0.75 miles inland from the edge of modern Kirkcudbright. This was traditionally the principal residence of Fergus, Lord of Galloway until forfeiture by Malcolm IV in 1160, and was probably thereafter used at least intermittently by his son Uchtred (killed in 1174). The larger of the two mounds - 'Palace Isle' - may have contained a substantial early hall-house. There was probably no occupation after the later 12th century; although archaeology could prove otherwise, and tradition connects the site with the

MacLellans of Bombie in the 16th century. Later agricultural and quarry use over the centuries have since obscured any discernible pattern of earthworks or foundations. However, the smaller of the two sites, the ancillary sounding 'Stable Isle', shows footings of an oblong structure. There are clear indications of a former causeway. Obvious comparisons exist with other Galloway island 'castles', notably Lochrutton and Loch Maberry.

Parton motte (NX 696697) and 'Boreland of' (NX 693709)

Overlooking Loch Ken and providing a classic medieval-fief pairing with the adjacent kirk (oldest surviving portion 17th century) is another undocumented but probable late 12th century motte. Having retained its original (pudding-bowl) shape fairly well, the summit now measures approximately 15m in diameter, being some 8m in height, above a ditch 7m wide by 1m deep. Mature trees cover both motte-summit and ditch. No apparent traces of a bailey are evident; but the adjacent (now disused) railway line has clearly disturbed the ground on the E, with moreover the field on the other sides having been cultivated for centuries.

Less than a mile NW of the motte is another obviously altered natural feature - here a rocky eminence above the Boreland Burn. A ditch cuts the feature in two, suggesting a crude form of motte-and-bailey. And while it may represent a subdivision of the original fief (possibly by the early 1200s), equally it may date from an earlier, or even later, age.

Shirmers Tower (NX 657742)

An ivy-clad fragment standing on a high bank represents a tower-house built by the Gordons of Kenmure, and apparently burned-down in 1568.

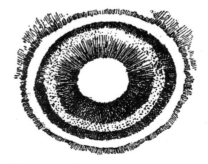

Parton, 19th c. elevation and plan

Southwick motte (NX 936570)

Beside a burn is a low (2m high) motte with a summit diameter of approximately 20m. Slight traces of a ditch remain. Aerial photography has found evidence for a bailey to the W. Edward I visited the church of Southwick in 1300, fragments of which survive at Old Southwick Churchyard. The motte may have been constructed by one Gilbert fitz Orm, son of Gospatrick who held adjacent Colvend. By the time of Edward I's visit the lord of Southwick was another Gilbert (a direct descendant?) 'de Suthayk'.

Threave Castle (NX 739622)

Probably Galloway's best known castle, maintained by Historic Scotland (who provide a boat service to the monument) and its predecessors since before World War I. Threave combines impressive remains with both an evocative setting and a history of national importance. In brief, the castle consists of a huge (now roofless) late 14th century tower shielded on two sides by a mid-15th century artillery fortification and water-filled moat. Outwith the moat are footings of a former hall and other service buildings, these revealed by late 1970s archaeological excavation. The whole ensemble is set on an island on the River Dee (particularly wide and marshy at this point). Almost unique, a defensive harbour (entered through a wooden gate, and overlooked by a D-shaped stone wall) was revealed. The tower itself was built by Archibald 'the Grim', 3rd Earl of Douglas, probably soon after he was granted the revived Lordship of Galloway in 1369. However, like regional magnates elsewhere (including previous lords of Galloway) Archibald's 'Black Douglas' descendants became too powerful (and self-willed) for royal liking; and in a mid-15th century wider suppression of the Douglases Threave was eventually captured and retained by the Crown (though later given to the Maxwells). A peaceful history then ensued until the Bishops' Wars of the late 1630s, when the Catholic Maxwells held Threave for King Charles I against forces of the Scottish Covenanting regime. After a thirteen week siege, the castle surrendered and was slighted, though was patched up in the 19th century to house French prisoners of war.

Standing to four storeys below a battlement - the crenels of which were dismantled c.1640 but whose put-log holes (formerly supporting overhanging defensive hoardings) are evident - the entrance was originally placed at first-floor level (later lowered to the entresol, or upper ground-floor) and given the added protection of an overhead machicolation. Above a vaulted ground-floor, the hall contains a sizeable but now-featureless fireplace, large windows now minus their seats, and the former entrance later converted to a window. The screening artillery defence is a monument of national importance in its own right. Representing the first such undertaking in the country, its low and sloped walls and three towers carried gun platforms, and are provided with large 'keyhole' gunports.

Whinnyliggate 'Camphill' (NX 717519)

An apparent moated-manor, of which typically nothing is known. It consists of a ditch surrounding a near-rectangular area measuring approximately 55m by 35m.

Wreaths Tower (NX 952565)

Only a fragment of corner wall (containing the base of a turnpike stair) remains from a tower-house built by the Douglas Earls of Morton sometime in the early 16th century.

Other probable moated-manor sites include Crogo (NX 758774) and Meikle Spyland (NX 714518); in Western Kirkcudbrightshire, suggested castle sites at Manor (NX 654444) and Nunton (649496).

Postscript

Recent decades have witnessed the restoration, in some cases a sensitive part-rebuilding, of several tower-houses prior to re-occupation as private homes. At the time of writing, Barholm is the most recent member of the group. Others include Barscobe, Cassencarie, and the Old Place of Monreith. Yet almost in a postscript to the castle story, Galloway's first 'new' tower-house recently appeared just within the northern boundary: Brockloch Tower, north of Carsphairn village, on the W side of the A74. A white harl covers modern construction materials. But the distinctively Scottish flavour imparted by a combination of crowstep-gabled attic, 'pepper-pot' corner turrets, and a generally sentinel-like appearance, recall an era of four centuries and more ago - and surely presents a more interesting spectacle to the passing motorist than would most modern bungalows.

Brockloch Tower

Bibliography

Barrow, G.W.S. *The Kingdom of the Scots* (2nd edition, Edinburgh University Press 2003).

Cruden, S. *The Scottish Castle* (Edinburgh, 1960).

Gifford, J. *The Buildings of Scotland: Dumfries and Galloway* (London, 1996).

Gourlay, R. & Turner, A. *Historic Kirkcudbright: the archaeological implications of development* (Scottish Burgh Survey, 1977).

Gourlay, R. & Turner, A. *Historic Dumfries: the archaeological implications of development* (Scottish Burgh Survey, 1977).

Harper, M. *Rambles in Galloway: Topographical, Historical, Traditional and Biographical* (3rd Edition, Dumfries, 1908).

MacLeod, I. *Discovering Galloway* (Edinburgh, 1986).

McGibbon, D. & Ross, T. *The Castellated and Domestic Architecture of Scotland*, 5 vols (Edinburgh. 1877-82).

McKerlie, P.H. *History of the Lands and their owners in Galloway* 5 vols (Edinburgh, 1870-78).

Oram, R. *The Lordship of Galloway* (Edinburgh, 2000).

Stell, G. *Exploring Scotland's Heritage: Dumfries and Galloway* (RCAHMS, 2nd edition, 1996).

Tabraham, C. *Scotland's Castles* (London, 1997).

Tabraham. C. 'Norman settlement in Galloway; recent fieldwork in the Stewartry', in D. Breeze (ed.), *Studies in Scottish Antiquity Presented to Stewart Cruden* (Edinburgh, 1984).

Yeoman, P. *Medieval Scotland: an archaeological perspective* (London, 1995).

Young, A. *Robert the Bruce's Rivals: The Comyns (1212-1314)* (East Linton, 1997).

Reference works:
Royal Commission on the Ancient and Historical Monuments of Scotland, Inventories for *County of Wigtown* (1912), *Stewartry of Kirkcudbright* (1914), *County of Dumfries* (1920).
The Archaeological Sites and Monuments of Scotland, 26: East Rhins (RCAHMS, Edinburgh 1987).
The Archaeological Sites and Monuments of Scotland, 24: West Rhins (RCAHMS, Edinburgh, 1985).

In addition to the above, the online RCAHMS databases provide an invaluable source of, in particular more recent, detail on individual sites; this especially so with regard to any archaeological excavations and/or surveys conducted in recent decades; however architectural descriptions are also frequently provided, along with some historical information.

*Balgreggan motte
(see page 30)*

*Abbot's Tower
19th Century sketch,
MacGibbon & Ross
(see page 30)*

Western Galloway

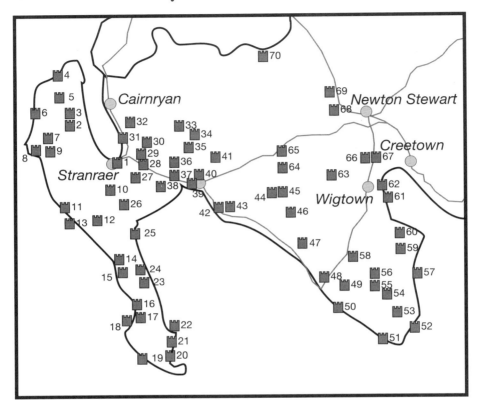

Rhins

1. Stranraer St John's
2. Craigoch
3. Marslauch
4. Corsewall
5. Balsarroch
6. Castle Ban
7. Isle of Lochnaw
8. Galdenoch
9. Lochnaw
10. Kilhilt
11. Dunskey
12. Kildonan
13. Dunaldboys
14. Low Ardwell
15. Killaser
16. Balzieland
17. Glen-of-the-hole
18. Clanyard

19. Auchneight
20. Broadwall
21. High Drummore
22. Drummore
23. Auchness
24. Ardwell
25. Balgreggan
26. Garthland
27. Freugh
28. Cults
29. Inch Crindl
30. Castle Kennedy
31. Innermessan
32. Craigcaffie
33. Larg
34. Balneil
35. Old Halls of Craig
36. Round Dounan
37. Dunragit
38. Droughdoul
39. Castle of Park
40. Glenluce

Machars and Penninghame
41. Carscreugh
42. Sinniness
43. Auchenmalg
44. Mochrum Castle Loch
45. Old Place of Mochrum
46. Crailloch

47. Druchtag
48. Myrton
49. Old Place of Monreith
50. Barmeal
51. Castle Feather
52. Isle of Whithorn
53. Whithorn
54. Castlewigg
55. Ravenstone
56. Drumgin
57. Cruggleton
58. Longcastle
59. Old Place of Broughton
60. Sorbie
61. Baldoon
62. Wigtown
63. Clugston
64. Mindork
65. Craichlaw
66. Penn. Bishops' Palace
67. Clary
68. Skaith
69. Castle Stewart
70. Loch Maberry

Eastern Galloway

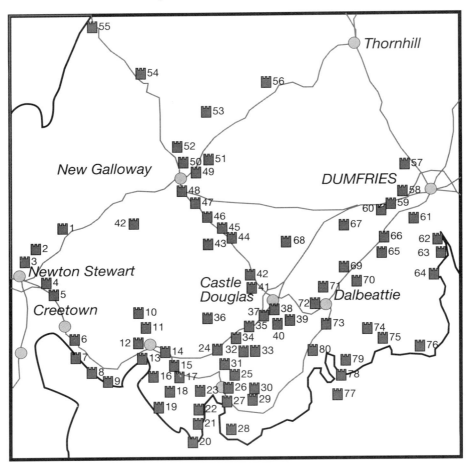

1.	Old Risk	9.	Kirclaugh
2.	Garlies	10.	Rusco
3.	Minnigaff	11.	Pulcree
4.	Larg	12.	Cardoness
5.	Bardrochwood	13.	Anwoth
6.	Cassencarie	14.	Cally
7.	Carsluith	15.	Enrick
8.	Barholm	16.	Plunton

17. Borgue
18. Barmagachan
19. Roberton
20. Manor
21. Balmangan
22. Nunton
23. Kirkchrist
24. Twynholm
25. Loch Fergus
26. MacLellan's
27. Castledykes
28. Dunrod
29. Bombie
30. Clownstane
31. Cumstoun
32. Meikle Spyland
33. Whinnyliggate
34. Culdoach
35. Netherthird
36. Trostrie
37. Kirkcormack
38. Auchlane
39. Ingleston
40. Gelston
41. Threave
42. Greenlaw
43. Little Duchrae
44. Parton
45. B. of Parton
46. Burned Island
47. Shirmers
48. Kenmure
49. Balmaclellan
50. Dalry
51. Barscobe
52. Earlstoun
53. Lochinvar
54. Dundeugh
55. Brockloch
56. Lochrinnie
57. Fourmerkland
58. Collochan
59. Lochrutton
60. Auchenfranco
61. Hills
62. Abbot's Tower
63. Ingleston
64. Kirkconnell
65. Corra
66. Drumcoltran
67. Milton Loch
68. Kirk. Durham
69. Edingham
70. Barclosh
71. Motte of Urr
72. Buittle (2)
73. Little Richorn
74. Auchenskeoch
75. Southwick
76. Wreaths
77. Hestan
78. Barcloy
79. Colvend
80. Orchardton

The Castles of Galloway